THE OTHER SIDE OF THE LOOKING GLASS

Adventures into Subtle Realms Around and Within Us

Paula Polson

First published by Busybird Publishing 2023

Copyright © 2023 Paula Polson

ISBN:
Print: 978-1-922954-62-6
Ebook: 978-1-922954-63-3

This work is copyright. Apart from any use permitted under the Copyright Act 1968, no part of this publication may be reproduced, stored in a retrieval system or transmitted in any form or by any means, electronic, mechanical, photocopying, recording or otherwise, without the prior written permission of Paula Polson.

The information in this book is based on the author's experiences and opinions. The author and publisher disclaim responsibility for any adverse consequences, which may result from use of the information contained herein. Permission to use any external content has been sought by the author. Any breaches will be rectified in further editions of the book.

Cover Image: Paula Polson

Cover design: Busybird Publishing

Layout and typesetting: Busybird Publishing

Busybird Publishing
2/118 Para Road
Montmorency, Victoria
Australia 3094
www.busybird.com.au

Also by Paula Polson (nee Hart)

The Way Home – a Pleiadian Life-line for Humanity in Crisis
Riding the Change – Navigating Unprecedented Times

Contents

Preface i

PART ONE
Encountering the Animated Consciousness in Everything 1

CHAPTER 1 - Preparation 3

CHAPTER 2 - Finding Feng Shui 19

CHAPTER 3 - The Magic Starts 30

CHAPTER 4 - Nature Speaks 48

CHAPTER 5 - Extraterrestrials and Light Downloads 56

CHAPTER 6 - Initiations, Miracles and Time Warps 67

CHAPTER 7 - Pure Energy and Tantalizing Travels 80

CHAPTER 8 - Ghosts and Dark Nights 96

CHAPTER 9 - Peter's Confusing Magnetism 106

CHAPTER 10 - Decoding Masters 121

PART TWO
The Search Inner and Outer   127

CHAPTER 11 - Adventures in Paradise   129

CHAPTER 12 - The Nature of Reality   147

CHAPTER 13 - Feng Shui, Children and Pets   161

CHAPTER 14 - Ecstasy and Sudden Change   176

CHAPTER 15 - Miracles and the Sanity of Dogs   190

CHAPTER 16 - From Manhunt to the Infinite   201

CHAPTER 17 - A New Challenge and Taking Stock   216

CHAPTER 18 - Resisting Being   236

CHAPTER 19 - Living the Mystery   254

Preface

This book is an avenue into the magic and infinite possibility of life. Life is not bound by the rules we are taught. These teachings create the mindsets which birth boundaries and limitations, and the often dubious actions arising from them. This book aims to set free those mindsets through a recognition and celebration of the interconnected mystery into which we are all woven.

These pages contain a bouquet of experiences and thoughts, scented with poetry, intuitive writing and quotes. Some of the stories told here may be hard to believe, but they are all true and unembellished. My work as a feng shui consultant provided me with numerous demonstrations of the subtler secrets of life and many are shared in these pages.

Please note that the intuitive writing offered here was pertinent to me at the time of receiving it, and may or may not resonate with you at the time of reading. Spiritual evolution proceeds in an orderly fashion and is always moving forward, no matter how it may seem at the time. I hope the trajectory of the words in this book follow a similar path in the mind of the reader.

Preface

Many of my experiences seemed to me unusual and inexplicable. However my wish is that in reading about them you, the reader, will be reminded of experiences of your own and of their inherent mystery.

Most of all I hope to convey that all phenomenology is one, eternally arising from the infinite sea of consciousness of which we are all made. Included in the one consciousness is the whole of science, natural disasters, medicine, political systems, tyrants and heroes, plants and humans, electromagnetic fields, atom bombs, herbal medicines and chairs. Nothing is separate at all. There is one play playing, viewed from nine trillion pairs of eyes, as well as the uncountable unseen eyes around us.

Life has shown me again and again that consciousness speaks through all life forms and even elements. That all therefore matters, even if its form is temporary. Animals, birds, insects, trees and plants have demonstrated compassion, oneness and intelligence to me so often. All is consciousness dressed as form.

Names and addresses of clients mentioned in the book have been changed for privacy reasons.

If this book had a musical accompaniment, it would be the music of Ludovico Einaudi. I find in his music an exquisite simple reflection of the true colours of life.

My sincere hope is for your enjoyment of this book, and your recognition of yourself in it.

The Greatest Show on Earth

Roll up, roll up, come one, come all
Come see the show, and be enthralled!
There's every colour, taste and sound
You'll be amazed at what you've found!

It is the greatest show on earth
Your ticket came with you at birth.
You'll have five senses to explore
And with some luck, maybe some more.

The stage props change throughout your life
From Mum to dog, boyfriend and wife
As for the set - it varies so
Depending where you choose to go

Desert, forest, town or field
Each one has a different yield.
Even time is in this play
Seconds, minutes, hours and day.

You have a costume that starts small
And with the years grows big and tall
What starts as living entity
Becomes a fixed identity

That has its ways to play its role
Building character and soul.
This show of colour, form and space
It fascinates the human race

So taken up with every day
We quite forget we're in a play.
We think we are the dress we wear
And fear we'll die when it's not there.

This the greatest show on earth
Fills up our lives with pain and mirth
We are so much immersed in it
We only see a little bit

We miss the greater universe
And what may be even worse
We're ignorant of what we are
Each one a shining bursting star

We are awareness watching life
Living us - man, child and wife
Essentially we're all the same
One dressed as many playing the game

Life seeing itself in all its forms
Replete with oddities and norms
But that's the script behind the show
Come one, come all, we have to go!

PART ONE

Encountering the Animated Consciousness in Everything

CHAPTER 1

Preparation

*'The most beautiful emotion we can experience is the mysterious.
It is the fundamental emotion that stands at the cradle
of all true art and science.'*

– Albert Einstein

Into the Mystic

On that spring day I had a small outdoor table at a festival in the outer suburb of Berwick. Festivals were a good way to promote myself in my new business, and to spread understanding about feng shui, which was then still very new to Melbourne. At my table I had two chairs – one for me and one for anyone who might be interested in a short discussion or analysis of their floor plan.

The spare chair was unoccupied when a couple of women walked slowly towards me. The younger one was blind – an attractive young woman being gently guided by an older one.

They stopped at my table, so to engage them I remarked to the young lady, "You have a lovely brooch," to which she replied, "And you have a Chinese man sitting in your chair." She described his clothing, her description matching the clothing and hat worn by geomancers of ancient times.

Had I not been seated, I might well have fainted! That was the death of my scepticism about Hung, my unseen helper.

But I am racing ahead. I have not yet introduced myself. Perhaps I had better start closer to the beginning.

One of the reasons for this book is the extraordinary experiences I have had. Always a seeker of truth, at mid-life I seemed to have become a sort of mystic. Miracles, unbidden initiations, interactions with unseen realms, unusual powers and, among it all, a spiritual journey which led me to some exceptional people and mind-altering discoveries.

Maybe my life has been no more mysterious than yours, but it seems more inexplicable things have happened to me than to most people, and only decades later am I beginning to decipher some of them. My hope is that in reading the strange stories included here you will recognize echoes in your own life. We are all living the same mystery.

On our journey together I hope you have no objection to my having invited a few friends to join us. Einstein was a mystic, so he is coming along, as is Brian Swimme, the well known cosmologist; Adyashanti, an American spiritual teacher with a large global following; Bhagavan Sri Ramana Maharshi, the revered Indian Hindu sage; and Alan Watts, the English speaker, writer and philosopher. Of these, only Adyashanti and Brian Swimme are still in body, but they will nevertheless all have wise morsels to add to our conversation.

Before we fly off into the magical, allow me to introduce my family and early years, so you have some context.

A Silver Ribbon, Flying Ants and Fairies

We'll start with my birth in Cape Town, South Africa. According to my mother, obviously biased, I was a very considerate baby, arriving in the hospital at lunchtime on a Sunday. She too was considerate, refusing any drugs, to give me the best start in life. After the second world war money was tight, so my parents had concerns about affording a second child. At the time, my brother Michael was four and my father, Ted, was a newspaper journalist, who, like many of that ilk, liked a drink or two after work, which my parents could ill afford.

In her hospital room with me and her financial worries, my mother, Cynthia looked up and saw a silver ribbon of light in the room. On it was the single word 'YOGA.' This was 1949, long before yoga was popular in the West. Cynthia had no knowledge of yoga but took note, and serendipity did the rest. Soon after that a friend mentioned some yoga classics she might buy, and a small inheritance from a distant relative enabled their purchase.

In my early years, I was used to her telling me to pretend she was 'going to town,' as she was having her 'quiet time' and reading her 'holy books.' I was a quiet imaginative child and used these times to draw, write, be in nature and create all sorts of little things. The potting shed in the garden was cleaned up for me to use as a writing den, where copious stories of fairies were produced. I recall painting a pencil white and drawing tiny fairies all over it.

From a very young age I had a strong sense of the preciousness of this planet and all its wondrous creations. I used to rescue every one of the hundreds of flying ants that landed in my bathwater in summer. The thought of any of them drowning was unbearable, so they would be fished out by a finger one by one, and put on the side of the bath to recover. Most of them probably met their maker from their maritime exploits, despite my ardent efforts!

Desperately shy, I dreaded parties and tried to hide in my cup of school milk when my class sang happy birthday to me. My writing was appreciated at school but led to terrifying prospects. The teacher would announce, 'Tomorrow, Paula will read her composition to the class.' This inevitably led to a tummy ache the following day with the desired absence from school. The teacher would then call upon Beryl, the extrovert of the class who later became a well known actress, to read my story instead.

I was a firm believer in fairies and angels, and one night saw a beautiful angel with wings outspread, at the head of my friend Anne's bed, while staying the night at her house. I once thought I might have seen a unicorn too, behind a shop, but to be honest this may have just been wishful thinking.

Fortunately my parents did not dampen my sensitivity, and besides, I tended to keep these unusual events to myself.

The Reverent Mother, The Boring Teacher, Weird Hair and Visions

It was really later in life that the unusual began to happen, but a few incidents in my childhood stand out as odd.

While still in primary school I had a vivid dream of Jesus coming towards me across a field, his arms outstretched to embrace me. I turned my back on him and walked the other way. For years my behaviour in this dream baffled me, until I saw that in many of my past lives I had been persecuted or killed for being loyal to my religious beliefs. I entered this life with a sense of having been betrayed.

Looking back now over the past 70 plus years perhaps the general benevolence and magic of this life has been aimed at restoring my faith, which had been so battered.

My mother would speak reverently about certain people she knew as 'rather wonderful.' Although I never commented on this, as a child I was irritated by this reverence. There was an intuitive knowing that all people are equally wonderful and none should be singled out as special or revered. And I felt particularly annoyed that she clearly put these people above herself. I had no idea where this knowing came from, and didn't realize I was in esteemed company!

'Let every man be respected as an individual and no man idolized'.

– Albert Einstein

At about fourteen I was disconcerted to find I felt hatred towards our excruciatingly boring Afrikaans teacher. Her monotonous lessons seemed to last forever. Hatred was not a feeling I ever wished to harbor, so I prayed, just once, to be free of it. Immediately my feeling towards her changed to one of deep compassion. I realized that as a widow with two sons, she was so tired, having to drag herself through these lessons. It was not only the immediacy of my change in perception that astonished me, but the fact that from then on, whenever she addressed me in class, she did so with a new tenderness. Did she know what I had been thinking?

Teenage years meant enjoying the beach with friends; swimming and emerging with dripping, long hair. Friends looked at me with amazement as I combed my wet hair, asking why mine didn't tangle as theirs did. These were the days before conditioner was invented. I had no idea why, but ever since then my wet hair has tangled, just as theirs did. The idea had been implanted. How on earth did that happen?

When I read James Hilton's mystical book, **Lost Horizon**, about Tibet and Shangri La, I was captivated by a deep yearning to go to the Himalayas and discover the spiritual aura of the story myself. The other book that evoked a similar response was Somerset Maugham's **The Razor's Edge**, about a young, traumatized American pilot who set off on a journey to find the transcendent. He eventually met a guru in India who introduced him to Advaita Vedanta philosophy, and he became realised or enlightened. Part of the story is based upon Somerset Maugham's own meeting in India with the saint, Ramana Maharshi, who made a profound impression upon Maugham, as he did upon many.

At eighteen, while writing an English essay during my final school exams, I had a sudden, powerful vision of a world devoid of life. The earth was dry, barren and grey with tiny heaps of dust, many of which bore tiny webs. I had earlier had a vision of a world devoid of birds, which was bad enough.

These visions had a profound effect upon me and my life choices. I was determined to do what I could to ensure people would be sane enough to look after our beautiful planet, and not create this dystopian future. My appreciation of nature and of beauty caused the notion of losing the glorious variety around us to be unthinkable.

Perhaps these and other small events were the reason my life was filled with more questions than answers. I had a burning desire to understand how life worked, to peer behind the curtain and find the Wizard of Oz himself pulling the strings. And there was a deep sense of the sacred, of something profound, to be accessed especially in nature and contemplation.

Flamingos, a Typewriter and Spiritual Inclinations

My family were fairly intellectual – both parents highly principled and spiritually-minded in their own separate ways. On Sundays, my mother dragged my brother and me off to Sunday school, then in later years to church, while my father stayed at home. He contemplated life via T S Eliot, Carl Jung and other philosophical writers, in later life taking to Deepak Chopra.

In summer he often took Michael and me to the beach after we were released from church. There he would dive into the waves, surfing in on his thin, curved wooden board with great delight. On the way home, sandy, warm and happy, we would sometimes beg to stop at Rondevlei to witness the flamingo-covered lake. This was a breath-taking sight of jostling pink necks and long legs. Only occasionally would we be lucky enough to see them rise as one, turning the sky into a pink flapping phenomenon, with the beating sound of pale thunder.

My father also loved to bang out stories, poems and (later) letters to the newspaper editor on his big black Remington typewriter, when he wasn't working with that editor or actually administering the letters page himself. His puns in the newspaper headlines were legendary. Having beaten his smoking habit in middle age, he prophetically wrote a story called *Smokescreen*, about a time when smoking would be banned in public places, about fifty years before its time.

As a child I had no idea of the wisdom that lay behind my father's often used expressions of 'All is well' and, when asked about something still to happen,

'We'll see.' He wrote much poetry and obviously privately had his own powerful spiritual experiences. One poem was called *Rapture Now*.

My father's own father, Edwin, on retiring from his role as a journalist, had become an Anglican priest. Only recently, through Michael's family history research, did we learn of Edwin's sad start in life. When he was very young his mother had had a smallpox vaccination, which had given her, and many others, leprosy. She dared not touch her small son or let him use her towel. Soon she was sent off to the leper colony on Robben Island, where she spent the rest of her days; and where Nelson Mandela later toiled for twenty-seven imprisoned years.

Edwin's father then failed at a business venture and committed suicide. So the fact that Edwin rose to be editor of the main daily paper in Pretoria, was impressive.

Later in life, as my father and I walked together on one of my visits from Australia, he asked me if I thought there was a God, and admitted that he still didn't know, but said his prayers each night just in case.

While we soaked up the sun at the beach, my mother would be home cooking the Sunday roast lunch. She worked as a personal secretary, and her hobby and joy was gardening. Her gardens were marvelous creations of color and variety, from which she gathered flowers for decorating the church – dahlias, lilies, roses, spring bulbs and sprigs of prunus blossom.

She was quite psychic, reciting tales of ghosts she had seen in old houses growing up in England. In one family home she would regularly hear and see an old man join the family for breakfast. She sought guidance through spiritual pursuits such as her yoga books, and later New Age ideas; she learnt about crystals, natural remedies and meditated in a group.

From an early age I was advised to 'always listen to your little inner voice', and in times of difficulty, to 'rise above it'. In her upper class stiff-upper-lip English background my mother would have had to learn the hard way to 'rise above it', rather than indulge in emotion.

She was one of four siblings, and closest in age to Peter, who joined the navy and became a champion boxer. While still young, the resulting brain damage caused Peter fits of anger, violence and depression. So his father, Tom, gave up his medical practice and became a duck farmer, hoping this would take Peter out of harm's way. But while Tom and Barbara, my grandparents, were away for a few days, they received a postcard from Peter, informing them that by the time they returned he would have thrown himself under a train. This was no idle threat and the family were devastated by his loss.

One day soon after that Barbara suggested to Tom that they should go to 'sunny South Africa' and make a new start. So my teenage mother left all she had known and came to Cape Town with her parents, in an attempt to escape their grief. Peter's suicide was buried as a family secret, which my mother only related to me in my teenage years.

Like most of their generation, both my parents were involved in World War 2. My father, a sensitive soul who sent my mother poems from Cairo, was traumatized by his experiences in the trenches. My mother enjoyed much of her time in the meteorological division of the air force, flying in open aeroplanes with daring young pilots, who performed loop-de-loops for fun between taking measurements.

So they had both encountered personal trauma in their early lives, and maybe this is what drew them to investigate the spiritual side of life. Before they had children, my parents were part of the Moral Rearmament movement (MRA) – an international moral and spiritual movement founded in 1938. They were also interested in the healing methods of Joel Goldsmith, who authored many spiritual books including *The Infinite Way*.

When I turned sixteen, my mother took me to a mosque, a synagogue and various church denominations, then told me, to my relief, that my spiritual life was now up to me. She would not be taking me to church any more. This was welcome news as I had better things to do on Sundays by then, like sleeping in or socializing with my school friends.

My spiritual inclinations were certainly there, but they were private. I trusted my own investigations and experiences more than any doctrine. I would work it all out myself in my own way. From early on I was more drawn to the mystical than the mundane. Small talk had never been part of my experience. It bored me and I didn't know how to do it. I wanted to know what was behind everything, I wanted to know the truth and I wanted to be wise.

Church only saw me again, occasionally, when I had my own children. After each sermon I came home livid, determined to confront the minister about the myths he was promulgating. I wrote lists of my various grievances. Why on earth would only 'believers' get to heaven? What about all the people who had never heard of God or Jesus? How unfair was that? How could they talk about a loving God on one hand then claim this injustice on the other? I never did bother to confront anyone. Instead I drifted further away from the church, determined to find my own answers.

When word of transcendental meditation came in 1973, I was intrigued, so my fiancee, Reg and I signed up. The inner experiences were soon expansive and blissful enough to hook me in. This seemed to be a way I could discover more about the workings of reality behind our world, so I practiced it religiously twice daily.

At this time *Supernature* by Lyall Watson rippled the reading world, and served to reinforce my reverence for nature and my intrigue about its secrets and possibilities.

I also delved into the works of Hazrat Inayat Khan about time, space and the infinite. His words ignited sparks of recognition and several poems sprang from my musings.

'Impossibility is only a boundary of limitation which stands around the human mind.'

– Hazrat Inayat Khan

Shutter

Man and time have in common possible infinity and infinite possibility -
Man for growth, time for eternity.
By dividing the presence of time into
Past and future,
Man has stunted his growth, and time's eternity.
For when he is not in the present
He is not;
And when he is here
His perception is clouded
By yesterday's breath and tomorrow's mists.
Perhaps now it is beyond man
To snuff that breath,
Clear those mists
And conceive of the timeless awareness
Of reality.

So far my life had given me little clue about the strange times to come. Apart from being fortunate, it was fairly ordinary. Kind parents and brother, university, work, marriage, and in 1977 migration to Australia. The material world was predictable and following 'the book'.

Reg and I moved from Cape Town to Melbourne, via an exciting month of trekking and hitchhiking in New Zealand. I taught psychiatric occupational therapy at a tertiary institute and Reg soon secured a job with an oil company. Within a few months we were transferred across the country to Perth. Here we survived on bread and water long enough to scrape together the deposit on a three-bedroom, cream brick house with a big garden near the wide blue Swan River, with its waddling pelicans and graceful black swans.

In 1979 my daughter began her journey into form, and when I was five months pregnant the first anomaly happened.

What IS Outside?

Reg was away on a work course and I was sleeping peacefully in our front bedroom. In the early hours I was woken up by a strange repetitive, electronic beeping sound coming from outside. This was prior to any common use of digital technology, and the only time I had ever heard such sounds were in movies about extraterrestrials and UFOs. So I was terrified they were coming to do something to my unborn child or to me. I lay there frozen, listening to this sound, which seemed to be emanating from just outside the window. It was like a little beeping tune, repeated over and over again.

Eventually I realised I would not be able to live with myself if I did not have a look. So I leant towards the curtain, intending to move it aside. Simultaneously there was a strong gust of wind, the curtain blew into the room and the beeping stopped. This was a windless night. My heart was racing. What else could it have been apart from a UFO?

In the morning I searched the front lawn for signs of burning or markings of any sort, but there were none. That night I slept at a friend's house, too frightened to sleep alone at home.

There was nowhere to file this experience, so it went onto a mental back shelf.

Life continued to flow quite predictably. First our daughter was born, then there was a move back to Melbourne, and soon after that our son entered the world. My meditation practice took a very back seat as Reg was often away on work courses. I was sleepless and exhausted, with no family or friend support, a bright toddler and a baby boy with wheat and dairy allergies, as yet unheard of by the conventional medical fraternity. There were no rice cakes or gluten free breads in those days, so I was forever baking with peculiar ingredients!

The Dream that Jumped and a Prediction

The years went by, carrying with them a return to work, a divorce and a house move. I now only had the children half-time, so was again able to devote more time to my other chosen pursuits. A year of metaphysical studies, a year attending a Jungian dream group, Reiki, shamanic weekends, homeopathy and so many other interesting facets to explore. I noticed that, contrary to popular beliefs, working on my energy field seemed to keep me healthier and more flexible, than working on my physical body. That was interesting and surely showed which one is the primary driver, I thought.

Then an intriguing incident happened in the Jungian dream group. We kept dream journals and each session one person would read her dream for discussion. On this particular occasion Sophia read out her dream, of a room.

As she described the dream contents of the room, one of the other participants asked her if there hadn't also been a green chair in the corner. Yes, said Sophia, there had been. I had heard of the collective unconscious, but this seemed very precise. A detail of one person's dream had landed in the mind of another days later! How did that work?

A friend and I enrolled in a psychic development course, led by two people who seemed suitably psychic themselves. After a few fascinating sessions, Ray took me aside and told me that while the rest of the class were doing the course for interest, my psychic skills would be essential for my future career. I was still working as an occupational therapist in the conventional medical system and viewed this prediction with polite scepticism.

It was not too long before Ray was proved correct.

Cast Adrift in the Big Wide World

A few years later, in 1994, the psychiatric unit where I worked was closed down and I was relieved of my job as an occupational therapist. This private hospital had long been embarrassed by our psychiatric unit. Maternity or cardiac units were so much more respectable! So the cardiac unit was extended and at last the hospital was free of psychiatry.

By that time I had been exploring many complementary health modalities and was finding the western medical system frustratingly narrow, and ever more reliant on chemical solutions with unwanted side-effects. I was aghast at the hypocrisy of a system that claimed to be evidence-based and scientific, yet that so obviously engaged in a process of trial and error when prescribing for patients. It seems hard to believe, but one psychiatrist actually had a little party with his patient and her anaesthetist, to celebrate her 50th ECT (electro-convulsive treatment, commonly known as shock treatment). When is it seen that something is not working? This woman was later found to have a brain tumour, which the psychiatrist then took to have been the cause of her depression. Most of us quietly assumed the ECT's had in fact caused the brain tumour.

My attempts to introduce some healthier complementary modalities into the patients' program were met with delight by them, but horror and resistance by the above-mentioned psychiatrist. He demanded to know the 'scientific proof' of 'those things with Asian names', which had been usefully employed elsewhere for thousands of years! I was told to stop and given a warning.

I had stuck my neck out before within that system. When a young woman of 23 was told she would need to be on antidepressants for the rest of her life, I was too disgusted to let that be. Inconspicuously I took her aside, suggesting she discharge herself and see a good naturopath instead. She did so, thankfully without giving me away, and a few weeks later I received a very grateful letter from her. She had followed my suggestion and was now fine, with no need for any medications. I was very happy.

A decade or two later, I was filling up the car at a petrol station when I noticed a woman looking carefully at me. When I went in to pay, she came after me. She had recognised me from all those years ago and wanted to thank me for 'altering the path of her life'. She had had no further bouts of depression.

So in 1994 when the psychiatric unit was closing, the time was right for my exit, but how was I going to pay the mortgage?

Reg, by now with a new wife, was working in human resources and had taught me the value of outplacement counselling, so I negotiated that as part of my retrenchment package. Thus began an interesting chapter of finding out about myself and my strengths, weaknesses and wishes. Forms were filled in, friends were interviewed, and eventually I had the parameters of what I would like and be good at, but with no hint of what shape it would take. I knew I wanted to work for myself, with people, in a variety of ways and settings, indoors and out, in some sort of therapeutic capacity.

I studied Chironic healing, a type of etheric healing, but felt no passion for it. However, just as when I had learnt Reiki, I was chosen as the model to have healing performed on me by the teacher. This probably removed much of the etheric dross I had picked up from working for years with distressed people.

Then a couple of new male friends and I planned a personal development clinic, where I would run the sorts of classes I used to run with my patients – stress management, relaxation, communication skills. This never took off. But again there was a serendipitous benefit in it for me. One of the men was a gifted healer and activated my kundalini energy during a healing. I had an experience of unusual energy and lights, and will never know if that activation had some bearing on later events.

CHAPTER 2

Finding Feng Shui

Spirits Choose the Woman in the Orange Top

Luckily I was able to pay off my small mortgage with the retrenchment money. I was still running hither and yon looking for a new avenue to follow, when around Christmas a friend suggested that we attend a spiritualist church carol service for fun. Neither of us had ever been to a spiritualist church before but we both enjoyed new experiences.

The hall was crowded and the service uneventful until the last part, when several members of the church were assigned to go up on stage. Here they delivered messages from the spirit world to some unsuspecting members of the congregation. To my astonishment, all four of them had independently picked me – the woman in the orange top! The message from them all was similar: that I must stop 'juggling plates', settle down and wait, because my future was assured and would soon become obvious to me. It was weird enough that they had all picked me and seemed to have some idea of my situation without me saying a thing, but I was later even more impressed to learn that one of the spirits they had referred to – a friend who I thought was still with us – had actually passed on.

In retrospect, this is where my life probably started becoming magical. The rules started to be broken in all sorts of ways and it was as if I was thrust on some sort of trajectory, which suited me, but was not of my making.

A Guardian Angel and a Chinese Master

I was in a casual sort of relationship at the time with a man called Mark. He was an interesting and broad-minded person, who had attended a men's group for years, worked as a consultant and clearly had a curious mind, as did I. For years he was to surface in my life like some sort of guardian angel at times of need. He told me he was going to study feng shui for interest.

"Feng what?" I asked. He explained the basics and, pricking up my ears, I decided to enroll in the course as well.

While attending the course I found myself red hot with recognition and excitement. This was clearly it! This fulfilled all my criteria and would be my future. Mark dropped out and I continued, learning as much as I could. Mark was also attending classes with a Chinese master who taught qi gong, and he suggested maybe I should do so too. Tong took one look at me and proclaimed I had a pillar of light coming from the top of my head, so she would start me at level three!

I learnt mantras and mudras to clear past lives, protect me and increase my power and my feng shui effectiveness in various ways. These were secret and powerful and I was not meant to write them down, but on learning about my woeful memory, Tong relented and allowed me to write most of them in a special small book, which I still have. I will never know the effect of these mantras, but I repeated some of them thousands of times, and used the clearing and protective ones later during the first years of my feng shui work.

The Weeping Wife and the Friendly Hoarder

Feng shui felt like the proverbial home-coming. The more I learned about this ancient system of knowledge, the more some of my life experiences made sense. I had not realized how flavoured and skewed our lives are by the energies that surround us. They may be affected for better or worse, due to the history of the place, the architecture, the lie of the land and many other seen and unseen influences.

Shortly after my marriage to Reg, we had bought a sweet house in Cape Town. This was during the cruel days of apartheid, and we bought in one of the few multi-racial areas. Here I received one of my most cherished compliments. On a sweltering 40 degrees Celcius day I was laying bricks to make a new front path, while a young man lounging against the front door opposite, smoked and silently watched me. Eventually he declared he had never seen a white woman work so hard in his life!

Our little garden was delightful and the house perfect, yet whenever Reg was out I found myself weeping inconsolably in the bedroom. I had no idea why and assumed it had to do with my work with alcoholics, who carried much emotional baggage. I never connected my tears with the young couple who had sold us the house. They were going through the agonizing process of losing their adored two year old daughter to leukemia. At last I understood that my tears had been the expression of their grief, still hanging heavily in the memory of the bedroom.

When we moved to Melbourne we bought a house in Camberwell from a friendly elderly lady, who had crammed the passages with endless boxes of goods and was ever collecting more! The blocked flow of the house had replicated itself in her joints, which were stiff with arthritis. I had lived with scant possessions quite happily until then, but found myself more and more often meeting her at garage sales and fetes. We were soon swapping viewings of the treasures we had bought! I didn't realize until that feng shui course how much my behaviour had been influenced by the hoarding energy left in the house.

So often, I later found, those qualities and traits we assume to be 'just us', are actually merely a mirror of the energy in which we find ourselves. We are influenced for better or worse all the time by our surroundings, and are usually totally unaware of it.

Shadows in the Garden

There are shadows in the garden indeed, my friend.
Glimpse them as they flit past your averted gaze,
Catching your starlight and turning it into cold pudding,
Frosting your dreams with silver.
We live in a web of their silent making
Oblivious of our tortured dance
To their siren songs.

New Skills – a Pen and a Pendulum

During the feng shui course, there were two particularly formative events. One was meeting Karen, a classmate a few years younger. Our mutual interest in health and complementary modalities helped forge a quick bond, and she taught me how to do intuitive writing. This skill was to play an important part in my life in many ways, and it still does at times. It seems to provide a structure within which wisdom can come forth telepathically in response to my questions, as I write.

As time went on and my consciousness expanded, the quality of messages received differed, even at times conflicting with earlier information. Over the years I learnt that different levels of consciousness require different relative truths. Intuitive writing, or channeling as it is sometimes called, is available to anyone who opens the door to the wisdom surrounding us in the unseen levels of consciousness. Having led me to this valuable gift, sadly, within six months Karen had died of breast cancer, refusing treatment.

The other skill that changed my life was dowsing. Dowsing has been used for centuries, and is now even employed by industry, including mining companies. Water divining, often using willow twigs which point down when over an underground water vein, is possibly the most well known of dowsing uses and methods. Dowsing can be used to find many things that are either underground or invisible to us. It can also be used to obtain answers to questions.

I had made a vague attempt to learn this skill several years before, but my scepticism had got in the way. Now, it seemed, the time was right, and I, along with all others in the class, learnt to dowse. We used pendulums or bent wire to get answers, and to find underground water and other unseen phenomena. I recall my fellow students and I dowsing each others' energy fields.

My intuitive writing, which I soon called channeling, was most helpful. I would sit at my computer with questions, and listen inwardly for an answer. Initially I felt it important to know who was giving me the answer. Later, realizing we are swimming in a sea of intelligence which we tap into when doing this kind of writing, I did not ask for names, instead learning to resonate with what was true.

One of my early correspondents was White Eagle:

> You are being challenged by a great deal of uncertainty. Your lesson now is flexibility. You need to learn to roll with the thunder, drop with the rain, move with the wind. Life was never static - it only seems so if you cut yourself off from the elements.
>
> Your lesson is about being you, and you are intrinsically not separate. Your spirit is a part of others, and of the elements and the earth. Nothing is separate from you. Therefore what is your doubt? You cannot lack because you are abundance, unless you cut yourself off from it.
>
> We are sad to see so many people living like closed off islands, not realizing the potential they have for expansion and abundance. We would like to see them throw off their chains - the chains of mental limitation. Use your mind for your present experiences and your dreams, but keep them open-ended.

What the Blind Girl Saw

The combination of my psychic skills, intuitive writing and dowsing all played their part in a small but surprising event one spring day.

Quite soon after starting to consult in feng shui, I found that with the aid of information via the dowsing rod, at times I seemed to be contradicting what I had been taught, or going beyond it, yet achieving good results for my clients. This puzzled me, so I sat down at my computer to do some intuitive writing and find out more. What I found was a rather elaborate story about a Chinese geomancer from a long gone dynasty who had known me in that life, and was helping me with my career in this one. While in a way it made sense, my sceptical buttons were pushed on to red alert, and I thought I had better withhold judgement about whether it could be true.

Then came that spring day in Berwick, where a young blind woman saw Hung sitting at my little festival table! She had known nothing about my intuited story. That was the death of my scepticism about Hung, my previously unseen helper.

The Professor and the Map

The end of my scepticism about dowsing came about another way. A friend and I were both single parents and both concerned about financial security. After a few seminars and much thought, we decided investing in property was the way to go. Jen taught at a Technical College and promised she would find out from a professor there which suburbs were most likely to soon escalate in value. Meanwhile on impulse one day I decided to use the Melways (the Melbourne street directory) and my dowsing rod to the same end. According to my dowsing, the best suburbs to invest in were Thornbury and Coburg. As I had never heard of Thornbury, I was doubtful and put it to the back of my mind.

A few days later Jen rang and said she had the answer from the professor, who knew all about the property market.

"What did he say?" I asked with bated breath.

"Coburg and Thornbury," was the answer I heard, as my jaw dropped.

On that basis I bought my first investment property in Thornbury, and believed my dowsing rod in the future.

Bowing to the Wire

> Channeling: You know that the mind is a clever trickster. You know that awareness is quiet and underlies the noise of the mind. Do you always want to listen to the noisiest one, or would you choose to encourage the quiet one, by paying attention to it despite the clamour? The noisy one has nothing new to say - nothing surprising or of value. You have been hearing it all your life. The quiet one on the other hand can introduce you to constant magic and revelations beyond your imagination. So which one would you choose to listen to?

Truth be known, I had almost left the feng shui course halfway through. Doubt had assailed me, and I meant to quit the whole endeavour, as it seemed impossible to acquire enough of such a complex field of knowledge after such a short course. By this time, however, I had discovered that my dowsing rod was a very useful instrument in helping me make decisions for the best. I was determined to stop attending the course, but the dowsing rod seemed equally determined that I should attend the next day's field trip to some sacred sites. Thank goodness I bowed to authority in the form of bent wire!

We were asked to have an agenda about which we could seek guidance. That was easy. My heartfelt request was for direction. Was feng shui to be my future or not? Our outing to sacred sites was pleasant and interesting, on various rocky outcrops and mountains, but nothing much seemed to happen for me.

The Prophetic Orator

However, maybe this request at the sacred sites did have a bearing on events in the following days. Chief Seattle's famous and sadly prophetic speech came my way and I read it at the dining room table, and wept. He had made this speech in 1854 in response to the Governor's proposal to buy the indigenous peoples' land and provide them with a reservation. It was a long speech, which over the years has been variously interpreted. These excerpts represent the tone of it:

'How can you buy or sell the sky, the warmth of the land? The idea is strange to us. If we do not own the freshness of the air and sparkle of the water, how can you buy them? Every part of this earth is sacred to my people. Every shining pine needle, every sandy shore, every mist in the dark woods, every clearing and humming insect is holy in the memory and experience of my people. The sap which courses through the trees carries the memories of the red man. The white man's dead forget the country of their birth when they go to walk among the stars. Our dead never forget this beautiful earth, for it is the mother of the red man. We are part of the earth and it is part of us. The perfumed flowers are our sisters; the deer, the horse, the great eagle, these are our brothers. The rocky crests, the juices in the meadows, the body heat of the pony, and man – all belong to the same family.'

'The rivers are our brothers, they quench our thirst. The rivers carry our canoes, and feed our children. If we sell you our land, you must remember, and teach your children, that the rivers are our brothers, and yours, and you must henceforth give the rivers the kindness you would give any brother. We know that the white man does not understand our ways. One portion of land is the same to him as the next, for he is a stranger who comes in the night and takes from the land whatever he needs. The earth is not his brother, but his enemy, and when he has conquered it, he moves on. He leaves his father's grave behind, and he does not care. He kidnaps the earth from his children, and he does not care. His father's grave, and his children's birthright, are forgotten. He treats his mother, the earth, and his brother, the sky, as things to be bought, plundered, sold like sheep or bright beads. His appetite will devour the earth and leave behind only a desert.'

'You must teach your children that the ground beneath their feet is the ashes of your grandfathers. So that they will respect the land, tell your children that the earth is rich with the lives of our kin. Teach your children what we have taught our children, that the earth is our mother. Whatever befalls the earth befalls the sons of the earth. If men spit upon the ground, they spit upon themselves. This we know: The earth does not belong to man; man belongs to the earth. This we know. All things are connected like the blood which unites one family. All things are connected. Whatever befalls the earth befalls the sons of the earth. Man did not weave the web of life: he is merely a strand in it. Whatever he does to the web, he does to himself.'

I wept at the cruelty of colonialism towards indigenous peoples, and our blindness to our connection with nature and the Earth. Echoes of those early visions of a lifeless Earth played in my mind.

Feng shui is named after wind and water, and is about living in harmony with natural forces and the Earth.

Strange Happenings – a Box, a Feather and Animal Eyes

A couple of days later the doubts about my future ganged up on me again, and I found myself head in hands sitting at the dining room table literally crying "Help! What shall I do?" in sheer desperation. I just couldn't believe that after our course any of us would really be equipped to consult in this ancient and complex discipline, as much an art as a science. How could I earn my living this way? Karen had recently taught me intuitive writing, and I was trying to get answers from this.

Suddenly I had the strangest sensation of someone stroking my head comfortingly. Then of someone standing behind me. I looked around quickly but couldn't see anyone, yet the presence was still strongly felt. I sensed someone very erect, holding something, facing my back. At a loss as to what was going on, I asked my writing to explain. I was told that it was a native American who wanted to crack open the top of my head and pour the sacred contents of the box he was holding into me. Still not knowing what this was all about, but trusting it to be important, I agreed. Immediately I felt a strange sensation on top of my head, and then a pleasant trickling right through my body. After that I was informed, through my writing, to go to bed as I would have some important dreams.

The first dream involved a native American again, this time putting a small stone and a feather in my heart. I felt a rush of connection with the four directions, the seasons, the stars, planets, and the Earth. Then a second dream was a succession of animals coming up close to my face and looking me in the eyes – a bison, a cow, a lion, a buffalo. Their clear brown eyes were inches from mine and seemed to gaze into my soul.

After that I did not eat meat for thirteen years, until told to do so by a dentist in 2008.

Much later I was told that this initiation had been a result of the depth of my feeling when reading Chief Seattle's speech, and that he had been the tall figure at my back.

CHAPTER 3

The Magic Starts

Heart, Mind and a Special World

Soon after that, in 1995, I received more information from Chief Seattle via the intuitive writing:

> Go slowly as the eagle soars, forever watching from above, noticing every move below. You cannot do that if you are too busy with white man's affairs - in your mind or body. It is the time of much change. Mother Earth has had almost more trouble than she can bear, and much shifting of mens' minds must take place if Man is to survive at all. The die is caste. Change will go on, and become harder and harder to adapt to. Remember change will not affect you if you live in your heart. Nobody can take that away. It is a sacred place where no-one else can trample and intrude. Your heart is like one of the rocks on the earth - it belongs to itself.
>
> You must understand, things are not always as they seem. There are many mysteries which you are not meant to understand. But if

you flow with the changes, not seeking the answers, but accepting, your heart will be glad. It is your heart that matters, more than your head. A strong intellect can be good, but by itself can be dangerous. It is the heart that must find direction, and the mind can then be put in its service.

Do whatever you can to ensure your mother Earth survives. Our realms can do a great deal, but the fate of the Earth is still in your hands. There is not a long time to go before Mother Earth lifts up her arms and says, "No more – I can take no more." Appreciate what you have. Lift up your head and smell the wind, feel it caress your cheek. Feel the sun push the seeds up from under the ground, and the rain slake their thirst. Listen to the secrets of the rocks, feel the sap rising in the trees. This is a special world you live in.

How to live in your heart: You must be open like the wind, which is strong but gentle. It feels the shape of things and only moves what wants to move. Whatever it touches that will not move, it flows gently around. One can see right through the wind. It is only what it is – no more, no less. It does not choose to flow here round this one, and not around that one. It just flows where it must flow. The wind is wise. It changes only from itself. A big rock does not make it stop. It stops only when it is ready. To live in your heart is not easy, and yet it is the easiest way. Your head plays tricks on you and cannot be trusted. Your heart, if you are brave enough to listen to it, will always be true. Do not dismiss your mind. You need it – but it must be in service to your heart. It is there to help you find ways to follow your heart. Do not judge your heart by your mind. Rather judge your mind by your heart, for your heart is the wise one. Do not follow other peoples' judgements, as they might be coming from mind or fear. Your own heart is always the path for you.

After that strange initiation everything seemed to fall into place. I knew feng shui was the future for me. I became thoroughly convinced as to its efficacy through experimenting in my own home. These experiments started with my bungalow. I had had several overseas students staying in it, but had given the last one notice as he had been rude and inconsiderate. After that I was unable to attract another tenant, which was unusual, as the bungalow was private, surrounded by a pretty garden and usually sought after.

A Painted Bungalow, Chai Arrives and an Extraordinary Gift

Karen and I discussed this situation and decided that the previous tenant must have left some negative energy, which was unconsciously affecting would-be tenants. So we performed some ceremonies to clear away the old energy and I painted the outside of the bungalow, partly due to necessity, and partly to symbolically give it a new energy. To my amazement, on the day I completed the painting, a new tenant arrived – a young man from Thailand, by the name of Chai, whose grandfather happened to be both psychic and knowledgeable about feng shui!

The next experiment was to 'feng shui' my whole house. Over several weeks I put into action what I had learnt. Then I asked the dowsing rod what else needed doing. To my fascination, it led me to various pieces of furniture, directing me to swap items around in ways I would never have imagined. To clarify for those unfamiliar with dowsing: of course the bent wire could not speak. But when it had led me to a piece of furniture I would ask questions to get yes or no answers. A swing of the wire to the left meant yes and to the right meant no. (Should you try this, be aware the language of a dowsing rod differs from person to person.) If it was a yes to "Should I move this?", then I would ask to be led to where it was to go.

On the day I felt the task was completed, I met Chai's mother, Nin. She was in Melbourne for a quick visit from Bangkok, and told me over dinner that she was learning to read palms. When I shoved my palm in front of her and asked if feng shui was the direction for me, she declined, on the basis of lack of experience, and said I should come to her master in Bangkok for a palm reading. Not being flush with finances, I explained I would love to, but that this was not possible.

After her further persuasion and my further declining, Nin responded lightly that she would pay for the trip, it was nothing to her, and I must come and stay with them and meet her teacher. Having just completed the feng shui corrections to my house, my jaw dropped at this extraordinary offer from a woman I had only just met. My children and I were impressed! Feng shui is meant to bring one good luck – well it was certainly working!

After balancing the geomancy of the whole garden, where I had discovered fault lines and negative geomagnetic lines, new life was attracted too. I found a clutch of kittens under an azalea bush, and birdlife increased in the garden.

Then to add to my amazement, the following day my mother phoned me from South Africa to tell me about a suitable job opportunity which would present itself to me in Melbourne soon. This was completely out of character for my mother, who regarded business with mild disapproval and suspicion, saying it was all about, 'You scratch my back and I'll scratch yours!' She had met someone in Cape Town whose relative in Melbourne needed a health professional to help sell therapeutic mattresses. This part time job helped tide me over financially while I started my feng shui consulting.

A Magical Trip, a Master Palm-Reader and a Wicked Car

The trip to Bangkok did take place a few months later. It was like a fantasy. Nin and her husband Manit were impeccably generous and thoughtful. They lived in Chai's grandfather's house, surrounded by singing birds in hanging bamboo cages. This pious old man, an ex-police commissioner, meditated each morning in an upstairs room full of silver, brass and possibly gold Buddha statues facing east, then went to work with the king. He did not speak English but presented me with a delicate glass ship in a bottle to symbolize success in my feng shui career.

Manit and Nin took me to the famous and most humble palm reader, who told me, through their impressed interpreting, that I was psychic like him, and could do the same sort of work. He assured me that my house was good for me, but my car was bad, which certainly proved true. They took me to many fascinating places – the awe-inspiring King's Palace, and down the klongs with their ramshackle houses teetering over the water and their flower-vending boats. We visited exotic temples with massive golden Buddhas, where Nin instructed me, as I was no good at sitting cross-legged, let alone in the lotus position, that I must never sit with my feet towards the Buddha – always fold my legs back.

After entering one such temple, I was taken next door to the monastery to view the undecomposed body of a revered monk, who had died many weeks before. The fact that his body was not decomposing indicated a very unusual state of spiritual accomplishment. He peacefully lay enclosed in glass while we filed past him, alongside many devotees. As we left and were walking between the temple and the monastery, a young monk, his robes flying, came running towards us and humbly presented me with a gold clip with the revered monk's face in relief on it. My hosts told me this would bring me good luck. Maybe it brought the young monk good karma too! Despite many accidental washing machine misadventures and getting lost several times over the years, mysteriously that clip is still with me and as good as new. Maybe it has been responsible for some of my good luck – I will never know.

At another large temple there were beautiful Buddha statues on sale. The presiding monk tried his best to explain to me their significance, but I had no idea what he was saying until my hosts explained that these Buddha statues had been made from the temple tiles, which had been replaced. The tiles had been ground up and reformed, and the statues would therefore carry very beneficial energy. I bought two, one for me and one for a close friend.

On my return to Melbourne I tried to sell my car, which seemed intent on killing me! It repeatedly stopped for no reason while I was driving on busy roads. Three cars crashed into it: one from the rear at a red light, others from the side and front. When I decided to sell it, it sprang an oil leak. Eventually, while driving to the shops one day, I felt a small hate-filled entity trying to choke me. Aware there was really no danger on the material level, I logically worked out that the antidote to hate was love. When I beamed love in the direction of this little monster, it shrivelled like a popped balloon. After that there were no more car dramas and I sold it easily, assured that it would not give the buyer any similar problems.

The Ailing Hairdresser and the Plumber Who Changed His Mind

The Thai visit seemed to provide a spring-board from which my new career took off. My first client gave me added encouragement. Lyn, a friend of a friend, had begged me for help for her daughter, Beth, before I had completed the course. I had refused, feeling I knew too little, and referred her to someone more experienced, whose fee she could not afford. On my return from Bangkok, I told Lyn I could now help her.

The problem was Beth's hair salon, which had had a run of bad luck in the few months since opening. There had been two robberies and a flood, which insurance would not cover. Finances were getting very low and so was Beth's self-esteem. To make matters worse, Beth was in a relationship that did not seem to suit her. I visited the salon and the home, and the problem turned out to be at the house, not the salon. The home visit had to be cancelled once or twice as I was definitely not to be there when Bruce, Lyn's husband, was there. I was told he was a very sceptical plumber, and must not know about my visit. Ironically, when I eventually did arrive, he returned from work for a tool he had left behind, and found me there, candle and all. I continued regardless and he politely made no comment.

Where Beth slept I found a strong negative place memory, which had been affecting her life adversely. This would have been created by traumatic emotion or ongoing milder unpleasant emotions such as anger, grief or guilt at some time in the past. After this was cleared and other corrections were made in the house, the hairdressing business went from strength to strength; Beth's unsatisfactory relationship with her boyfriend broke up; her self-esteem improved; and Bruce won $1000! Lyn found a new career and spiritual interests, and to our great amusement, Bruce made sure no-one moved anything from its recommended position. Most of the family were then referred to me for feng shui services and my business was off!

My journey with feng shui was constantly fascinating and ever-changing. There are so many books on the mechanics of it, but few which relate personal accounts, and include the more psychic side of environmental energy work. So I offer you some stories in the hopes that they will fill a gap in the literature, but more importantly, that you will enjoy them and find them as intriguing as I found the experiences to be.

Feng Shui

Too eloquent a dance to be trapped in prose
To be defined by what one 'knows'

Before the phone call the weaving begins
Client weaves as practitioner spins

Fabric is formed as the process takes shape
Patterns part and molecules awake

Future and past each tell their tales
Present links both to cure what ails

Intentions lend the ethers flavour
Which (respected) spirits savour

A chaotic swirl of change
As settled elements rearrange

Moments of uncertainty
Shadows of doubt

Then Heaven descends
To meet the rising Earth

and

There is balance.

A Sad Farewell and Familiar Knowing

Not all feng shui consultations yield results as obvious and dramatic. I believe the first few were especially designed to encourage me. Sadly, at about the time of all this exciting change in my life, Karen discovered she had cancer. We also discovered she had been sleeping above polluted underground water, which is known to be a cause of cancer. It was too late for the correction of this to enable her recovery, and she died within months.

Looking back, I now understand why, at times, I used to get quite agitated about my environment. Certain things had to be certain ways or I would not feel settled there. My family had a strong unconscious sense of good feng shui, as do many people. I knew where there should be a fence or where it should be open; which rooms needed a touch of red and which should have none; and where the flowerbeds should go. Learning the rules of feng shui made so much sense, feeling familiar and right.

Many people have lost faith in their intuition, but it is always there, alive and well under the layers of rational, scientific thought that have been so encouraged by our society. So often I would advise a client to put a pot plant in a particular spot, to be answered, "Oh that's where it usually is. I just moved it this morning"; or recommend a certain colour scheme, to be told, "Isn't that funny – I had been thinking of those colours." So sometimes feng shui is a way of returning our faith in our own ability to know what works for us.

The Intuitive Wife

Ruth, a gently-spoken middle-aged woman, told me in the initial call that she would like to ensure 'things at home' were supporting the family as well as possible, and that since building an extension, she suspected they were not. She also mentioned her eldest son was 'a handful', and that she was not comfortable in her office. She warned me the house was large.

It was a rainy day when I drove up to the house in a prestigious Melbourne suburb. Entering the walled garden, I was struck by various well-placed large objects d'art. Square ponds either side of the front door interested me too. I wondered if they were suitably placed for feng shui. The placement of water is very significant.

After greeting the busily employed gardener, I rang the doorbell on a most imposing double front door. Ruth welcomed me, leading me inside. To my surprise, we passed an enormous, twisted, grey, metallic sculpture, about three metres high, and at least a metre wide, in the entry hall. Again, I couldn't help wondering if it was well placed for feng shui purposes.

I put my briefcase down at a suitable working table near the kitchen, then followed Ruth for the inevitable guided tour of the house. Ruth informed me that she and her husband liked to support the arts and were serious collectors. Paintings, sculptures, and elegant glassware had obviously all been placed with the greatest care to maximise their effect. It was quite an extensive tour this time – upstairs, downstairs, old section, new section. When we approached the new section upstairs, where the son's room was, I found the vibes were so bad I could not, or would not, enter. The feeling was dense and nauseating, and I found myself clutching my solar plexus protectively. I told Ruth I would have to retreat. We went back down the stairs, and instead went up the other, old staircase, to the old section, where the main bedroom was. There the energy felt fine. Then down to the office, where Ruth said she could not concentrate well, and felt there was a problem. It looked and felt okay to me at that stage.

Then the tour of the garden. There was a green-surfaced tennis court, lawns, a swimming pool, a porch, statues, pergolas, fountains; and attractive potted plants, trees and garden beds.

Having tried as best I could to take it all in, I sat down at the worktable, with the floorplan and the usual glass of water, while Ruth retreated to her office. She had mentioned that when they had built the extension, including her son's room, there had been much unpleasantness between the builder and the architect. I guessed this explained the awful energy up there, and the consequent problematic behaviour of her son.

My first task, partly so I could access that part of the house without ill-effect, would be to clear the energy field. This I did, plus a blessing on the house, which, as always, brought in a special additional quality to the 'cells' of the energy field. Then I was able to climb the stairs, enter the new wing, and feel no ill-effect. The rooms seemed fine structurally, apart from a few small problems of energy flow, which could be easily corrected by keeping certain doors closed.

So, back to the drawing board, and I began to work out the Flying Stars, the powerful astrological system often used in feng shui, which takes into account directions, time and elements. Based on the house building date and compass direction, I worked out what influences affected each part of the house, and how best to support or weaken these, depending on their usefulness.

"That's lucky," I thought, " The water pools at the front are both well-placed." I wondered again about the huge metal sculpture in the hall, only to find that the cure for this area was a 'a metal mountain', meaning, ideally, a tall metallic item of some sort. Perfect again!

"Where's their Water Dragon?" I wondered. This is the main wealth influence, which potentially brings wealth for a twenty year period, and should be supported by a water feature, with moving water. It was in the north. Looking in the garden in this area, I found, to my amazement, there was not only a small pool with a fountain, but that the water was spurting out of a dragon's mouth! It could hardly have been more appropriate.

Their Mountain Dragon, potentially bringing health for twenty years if supported by an earthy or metallic 'mountain', or tall structure, was in the north west.

"Ah!" I thought, "They need to install something here," only to discover they had already built a pergola, made of stone columns!

By now I was pretty impressed. These people were obviously extremely intuitive. They seemed to have done everything right, without knowing why they had done it. Adding to this theory, I discovered that in the north-east, where a body of water was highly contra-indicated, was their large pool, but they had shut it off from the house by means of a tall hedge, thereby rendering the water virtually harmless.

In the west, where the kitchen was, red was needed, to harmonise two conflicting elements, and thereby reduce the risk of problems for children. I looked up and saw not only bright red plastic chopping boards, but also a large red rubber overlay on the kitchen floor!

I was beginning to wonder if these people really needed my services, apart from the energy clearing, when Ruth appeared to ask how I was going. I told her she should be a feng shui consultant, and that almost everything they had placed in the house was perfect for their feng shui. She beamed, and said she found that most affirming, admitting that her husband often relied upon her intuition.

Then she told me of a day when the family had gone to look at a property with a view to buying it for the land. On entering the driveway, she had instantly felt it was unsafe, and had instructed her husband and children not to get out of the car. They had later found out that an isolated woman had died there, and that, over time, her undiscovered body had been eaten by her starving dogs. The energy of that place would probably have been ghastly. Ruth believed much of the family's good fortune had stemmed from honouring her intuition.

The problem with the office turned out to be one of electromagnetic fields from the power lines outside. Almost all the furniture was conductive metal, which added to the problem. No wonder Ruth felt tired and headachy there. We installed some gadgets to reduce the effect of the electromagnetic field, and I suggested a non-metal desk and chair.

Having discussed the few things which needed attending to, I warned Ruth that her son may become temporarily unwell as he 'detoxed' from the old bad energy in his room, which had now been cleared. After all, he had been breathing in that energy for a long time, each night and part of the day, and it would be almost as much a part of him as of the room. Now the room was clear there would be an imbalance – a mismatch between him and the room – and the natural tendency would be for his body to want to rid itself of the old energy, and create a 'clean slate' to match that of the room. I suggested she advise him to drink lots of water, and give him vitamin C.

I drove home that day reflecting upon the wonder of our intuition. It is there for us to tap into if we will, with so much otherwise inaccessible knowledge and wisdom.

Ruth phoned me a few days later to tell me that her son, notwithstanding the water and vitamins, had come down the day after the consultation with influenza-like symptoms. Again she seemed pleased, finding this quite affirming of the whole process.

Later she informed me that her son had changed markedly. He was calmer, seemed happier and was less demanding. This time it was my turn to be pleased. I may not have helped this intuitive client as much as I was able to assist others, but at least I had achieved the main objectives – a house that felt good, and a happier son.

The Desperate Doctors and the By-Passed Pharmacy

The man on the other end of the line sounded mildly embarrassed. He said he and his wife were both specialist doctors, into science and not given to superstition. They would not normally have called a feng shui consultant, but they were desperate and didn't know what else to do. I put aside my ego, which might have said feng shui is based on many sciences and arts rather than superstition, and listened to his story.

With the grandmother and their two young children, they had come to Melbourne from Singapore to stay for just one year. He was lecturing at a university and she worked as a surgeon at a large public hospital. Since they had moved into their house in Port Melbourne they had been having multiple strange problems. The fit and well grandmother had fallen down the stairs twice, and the wife once. The four year old had started to wet the bed and the baby had developed a weird rash. The heater made a strange noise and turned off repeatedly in the middle of winter, and there was also an icy cold area in the lounge. The wife was getting up to go to the toilet all night and couldn't sleep, and even the neighbour was oddly unfriendly and never greeted them. Overall they were having a pretty awful time and were mystified.

So on a sunny day in August 2005 I found myself driving along the clean streets of Port Melbourne, past rows of attractive houses until I came to no 30, The Boulevard. It looked like all the rest – tidy, newish and double-storeyed.

When I rang the bell, the door was opened by a dark-haired gentleman who courteously welcomed me and ushered me in. He was almost apologetic in telling me again about the trouble the family was having, and after I had off-loaded my bag and briefcase he showed me around. It was a typical well-designed townhouse – clean lines with plenty of white and beige. In the lounge I could feel the cold spot that he had referred to. Downstairs I could see nothing amiss superficially. The stairs were to the right of the front door and I was particularly interested in their configuration. People falling downstairs could indicate that the energy flow down the stairs was unusually fast, which can happen when staircases are straight and lead to a window or door. However this staircase was well-designed with a change of angle near the bottom. We had a look at the bedrooms upstairs and I was none the wiser. The doctor was wanting a quick consultation, not involving a floor plan or the astrology of the building. So all I could do then was tune in to the building and check the geomancy.

Using the dowsing rod, I located the omphalos, or energy centre of the house, sought permission from the house to tune in, and did so. Going through the list of possible earth energies yielded nothing, but what I then found made possible sense of all their problems. There were two earthbound spirits and one negative psychic impression.

Negative psychic impressions (NPIs), sometimes called ghouls, are formed by strong traumatic emotion, and need a steady stream of negative emotions to continue to exist. So they seem to have the ability to mysteriously create all sorts of havoc for people, in order to feed off the ensuing mayhem and misery. These incidents of misfortune are usually attributed to bad luck, or at times when fear is evoked, to ghosts. But they are very different from ghosts. There is no soul involved, though some form of intelligence seems to be invoked for self-preservation.

During my training we were advised not to interfere with them, but I found I could deal with them effectively, and had I avoided them I would have left many clients in difficult situations. On several occasions clients cancelled my visit the day before due to unexpected 'bad luck' – such as a car crash, a plumbing issue or illness. Often they would say they could no longer afford my services as they had to pay for this latest catastrophe.

After many such incidents I realized that these were all caused by NPIs who did not fancy me coming and dissolving them. I learnt to suggest to clients that we go ahead anyway, and that they could pay me later, otherwise the run of bad luck might just continue. Several times NPIs tried to prevent me from arriving at clients' premises directly. On the way to one house I kept getting lost in the most ridiculous ways. It was as though I could not think straight. On another occasion a car came straight towards me from a side street. Someone was certainly looking after me, as it screeched to a halt within a hair's breadth of my car. All of these premises involved one or more NPIs. It is a mystery how they work. The only possible way to explain how they knew when I was coming, or knew where I was, or what I would do to them, is the fluidity and all-pervasiveness of consciousness.

But, back to the doctors' house. Once I knew what I was dealing with, I felt some sense of relief that there was a probable way to resolve their strange mix of problems. The first step was to clear the energy of the whole house, then to dissolve the ghoul, which was at the bottom of the stairs. When I tuned into it specifically I felt the angry energy of a fight. It was particularly nasty and violent, but like all ghouls was essentially a memory superimposed upon an unchanging field into which it was then dissolved. The fight that had taken place at the time the ghoul was formed had claimed the life of one of the dock workers, and both dock workers were still stuck there in spirit.

People often believe that new buildings would not house ghosts, however often ghosts predate new buildings. Stuck in their time warp, buildings can in a sense come and go around them. I had an interesting case where a woman was having a house built, despite every tradesman involved making huge errors. She phoned me and expressed disbelief at the apparent stupidity of all involved. The final straw had been the roof. The builders had worked from both the left and the right, and when they reached the middle found the roof heights did not match.

What I discovered on site was the ghost of an intellectually disabled young man who had lived on that block of empty land. He was thrilled that someone was now apparently building him a house, so was helping all the builders as best he could! The effect on them of his consciousness mixed with theirs was disastrous for the job. By the time I arrived the house was almost complete, but after the disabled man had been sent on his way at least the last stage of building went smoothly.

Back to the doctors' house. The two tough and angry dock workers needed some help to finish their business and move on to a better destination. I then reported to my client that I had done what I could. I suggested he call me in a week or two to let me know of any changes.

In exactly two weeks I received a somewhat astonished call from the doctor. Every single one of their problems had corrected itself and no-one had fallen down the stairs. His wife was sleeping soundly, the four year old had stopped wetting the bed, the baby's rash had gone, the heater had become silent and was working, the cold spot in the lounge had gone, and to their final amazement, the neighbour had greeted them for the first time. He strongly suggested I go to Singapore, where I could easily make my fortune, and he admitted the whole experience had put a large dent in their scepticism.

This job was yet another lesson for me about the power of invisible forces over our lives. We really do live in a soup of factors which influence our minds, bodies and the course of our lives for better or worse.

Another simple illustration of this was a chemist shop in Coburg which I attended in 1997. Patti, the owner and pharmacist, told me she didn't understand why people did not enter her pharmacy. It was on a busy corner and she would watch people stride purposefully towards the door, then hesitate and walk away, time after time.

I stood outside for a while and noticed the same thing happening. When I tuned in I found there was the ghost of a drunk man leaning against the doorway. I told Patti this and she gave me a funny look, informing me that the shop used to be a pub. So even though this inebriate was totally invisible, at least half the would-be customers sensed his presence and were not game to barge in past him. Once he had been sent on, that was the end of that syndrome and customers entered smoothly.

CHAPTER 4

Nature Speaks

Trees that Scream, Plants that Feel and The Humble Worm

'Try and penetrate with our limited means the secrets of nature and you will find that, behind all the discernible concatenations, there remains something subtle, intangible and inexplicable. Veneration for this force beyond anything that we can comprehend is my religion. To that extent I am, in point of fact, religious.'
– Albert Einstein, 1927

My garden was my chief place of refuge, relaxation and creativity – my interest in gardening having been fostered by my mother's example and also by my primary school. At school, as part of our nature study curriculum, we had an annual excursion to the Kirstenbosch Botanical Gardens. These beautiful rambling gardens are spread over the lower slopes of Table Mountain and include a few picturesque, thatched stone buildings, one of which was for education.

Here we school children would sit wide-eyed, learning about nature. And here I learned from a wise woman, that when trees are cut down, one can sometimes hear them scream. That lesson has never left me. I learnt that plants and trees have an indwelling soul of sorts, or at least a nervous system, and can feel. This has been born out by numerous studies, as well as by my experiences. I recall visiting a house of two keen meditators, whose indoor plants were so huge and healthy they looked as if they were jumping out of their skins! The people attributed this to the vibrations of their meditation.

My aunt, who was not particularly into such things as plant communication, told me a story about a large daisy bush in her garden. She had recently been looking at it and contemplating taking it out. After that it started dying. She had felt so guilty she had reassured it that it could stay, and it had perked up again.

Sir J C Bose (1858-1937), an Indian polymath, physicist, biophysicist, biologist, botanist and author of early science fiction, invented an extremely sensitive instrument called the crescograph, which magnified the movement of plant tissue many thousands of times. He found plants were similar to animals in that they responded to stimuli appropriately. Through his experiments he found that plants have a delicate nervous system and feel a large range of emotions such as pain, pleasure, fear and joy. He also experimented with moving large established trees, and found they survived better if they were anaesthetised with chloroform before being moved.

In my current garden I inherited a lovely, big Japanese maple tree. To my dismay it started dying, branch by branch, and its trunk was cracked. Advice from others and from online indicated it had a terminal disease for which there was no remedy.

So I talked to the tree about how well it was doing, refusing to talk about the problem with friends in front of it. Instead I always spoke about how beautiful it was, and how healthy it was, and how it could get over any illness. It stopped dying back, amazingly grew a new trunk which almost encircles the old one, and now it is bigger than ever, in perfect health.

Our school nature study lessons taught me a deep appreciation of the wonders and preciousness of nature, for its own sake. I do hope that I am wrong in thinking that children are now usually taught about 'the environment' more from the point of view that if we don't care for it, it will be to *our* detriment. This is a rather different perspective, not inclusive of the love, awe, wonder and respect that nature deserves.

Ode to the Humble Worm

I may not look the best to you
I'm dressed in dirt and sticky goo
But listen to my story please
Let us briefly shoot the breeze

The thing is I'm a help to you
The reason why your garden grew
It is I who feeds your soil
You should be grateful for my toil

I burrow through and make tunnels
So air and water have good funnels
I chew the soil and spit it out
Feeding roots without a doubt

But here my tale becomes quite sorry
I must confide in you my worry
To build my house I simply dig
Your houses unlike mine are big

I cannot live under cement
When you construct we worms lament
There's nowhere then for us to go
And no room for your plants to grow

We know you like your houses large
No matter what the builders charge
But please recall there is more cost
Essential Nature's getting lost

We do hope you will beg our pardon
We liked the days when you had garden
When we could slide around below
As part of Nature's earthy flow

But now alfrescos steal our land
As houses outdoors too expand
This message we convey hereby
Is echoed by each butterfly

The birds agree and so do bees
That kindly pollinate your trees
Without them you would be bereft
So please consider some land left

Maybe we can live together
Share the space and share the weather
Houses may be very good
But humanity needs food

So when you plan to build your home
Please keep some clay and keep some loam
And plant a garden round about
So we can all enjoy being out

A King Tree, Flower Essences and Gardening by Dowsing

My friend, Anne and I once visited a nearby forest, and on tuning in to the trees I was intrigued to find that they each had a different persona. Some were welcoming and friendly, others not. Some exuded warmth, others coldness. The other interesting thing was that in this forest there was a balance. Near each tree would be its opposite in character. Near the 'king' tree of the forest was the 'queen' tree. Near a warm tree was a cold one.

My mother, who had read about Findhorn in Scotland, had told me it was a good idea to leave a small part of one's garden natural and undisturbed, for the nature spirits. I was not very good at this, but remembering what the Kirstenbosch teacher had said, I thought about the effect on plants of pruning. I decided I would warn a plant or tree before cutting any part of it, asking it to pull its energy down away from where I was going to cut, before I did so. If I was quiet and attentive, I could feel when the plant was ready. Even before cutting a bunch of flowers I followed this strictly for a few months.

During this time, a client who brought her daughter for a healing was quite breath-taken by the vibrancy of my garden.

"Just look at this growing, growing garden!" she exclaimed to her daughter.

However this considerate method of horticulture was extremely time-consuming, so eventually I only warned plants before major work. The garden reflected the change.

Having found flower essences to be a useful healing remedy for myself, I made dozens from my own garden flowers and each one told me what it could be used for. It was a simple process of leaving flowers on water in the sun on a warm day. Then the liquid went into small dropper bottles with a little alcohol as preservative. I often benefited from them, as did my dogs.

Once I had learnt dowsing, my dowsing rod became my chief garden assistant. If I wasn't sure of the priority, I would simply ask the dowsing rod what needed doing most in the garden, and it would lead me somewhere – to what needed moving, pruning, weeding or feeding. When I bought new plants and fruit trees, I asked where they would like to be planted.

At my new beachside house in 2008, I thought perhaps the dowsing rod was leading me astray when it indicated the place for my apricot and nectarine trees was right at the front of the property. I imagined my trees feeding all the passersby instead of me! Little did I then know that a year later I would be building a fence there, which would enclose my trees. The dowsing rod could read a future which my mind could not yet access.

Gnome Greetings and Invitations

The years of feng shui consulting brought me countless astonishing moments of magic and mystery. Perhaps thanks to a mother whose own experiences had opened her mind, perhaps due to many years of transcendental meditation and contemplation, or perhaps due to the grace of various initiations, my belief system was loose enough to allow an unusual range of other-dimensional and synchronistic experiences, which in turn served to expand my understanding of what we call reality. Many other realms became part of my experience at times: Pan, nature spirits, angels, extraterrestrials and occasionally ascended masters made themselves known to me, generally, but not always, in a helping role.

Nature spirits performed some mischief in my house to get my attention, then when told off, instead posed for me to draw them with my psychic vision. They dictated charming greeting cards I could make to celebrate such occasions as farewells, welcome, harvest, housewarming, parties, initiation, travel, promise and full moon.

Party invitation

I, the head gnome,
speaking also on behalf of the elves, pixies, and fairies,
invite you warmly,
and with the persuasion
of this small tankard of mead,
to join us in the merriment
of our forthcoming party.

You will find us at......................
at about the hour of......................
Please come warmly dressed if it is cold,
or coldly dressed if it is warm,
as we want you to be comfortable.

Please bring: A good story, a warm blanket, a jar of frogs for music, a friendly heart, dancing shoes, hazelnuts for bowling or belly laughs.

Appreciation

Tonight we the gnomes
will be holding
a feast of appreciation
in your honour.
We will sing
and dance
and lift up our goblets
in a toast to you.
Thank you.

House warming

We the house spirits of ....
are unable to do it on our own.
We need you to help us breathe
warmth, fun and festivity
into this new dwelling.
Please come at about ....
on ....
and bring with you
candlelight, soup, salt, bright colours,
flowers, fruit, a front doormat,
a dog, a cat, or a brown mouse.

One night they begged me to stop what I was doing – to join them outside under the moon for a dance. After all I had been through with invisible realms, I still doubted this enchanting request.

Midnight Invitation

On a cosy wintry night
Tucked in with books to read,
An invite from the fairy folk
To come and share some mead

"Come outside," they called to me,
"Let's dance under the Moon!"
"Am I making this up?" I said
And "It's cosy in my room."

But "Come outside," they called again.
"We've waited for you so long.
Let us jig beneath the moon
And sing a silvery song."

"It's so cold outside and I'm not sure
If this is all in my mind."
I stared into the dark outside
And politely declined.

"Come come come," they called,
"Let's share a drop of mead -
We'll sing until the sun rises
And the sky begins to bleed."

In case all this was happening
I briefly ventured out
And placed there a small cup of mead,
My head beset with doubt.

The calls grew silent right away -
They knew I'd not be drawn.
Come the morn I checked that cup
To find the mead was gone.

CHAPTER 5

Extraterrestrials and Light Downloads

The Sneering Man, the Tormented Cabbages and a Sweet Soul

In all those years of feng shui consulting I always felt safe venturing into the homes and workplaces of strangers. My simple belief was that as my intention was to help, life would protect me. Only twice was I not quite so sure about this.

At a large Mind, Body, Spirit Festival I was far from my little stall, chatting to another stall holder at the other side of the hall, when a tall strongly-built, dark-haired man approached me. With a thick accent, perhaps Israeli, he asked if I was the feng shui consultant. Surprised that he knew, as I was so far from my stall, I said I was. His reply was both challenging and somewhat sneering: "Let's see how psychic you are…"

Wanting to take control, I suggested we go to my stall, and there he towered over me as he booked an appointment for me to come to his home in a few weeks, on 6th of June 1996. His whole demeanour was threatening and I was well aware of the evil connotations of the number 666, so the prospect of venturing into his territory did not really appeal.

The weeks rolled by until the 5th of June. I was to visit him the following day. My phone rang. It was a woman.

"You have an appointment at ten tomorrow with Mr X," she told me. I replied I had an appointment but not with anyone of that name.

"He goes by several names," she said. "He cannot keep the appointment as his lawyers will be in town." I was somewhat relieved, but found myself telling her he would have to phone me himself if he wanted to cancel. This he did later in the day. Intuitively I knew it was crucial that I show no fear. We agreed he could ring me later to make another appointment if he wished to, but to my great relief, he never did. I felt life had stepped in to save me from something potentially sinister.

The next concern about my safety came a few years later, in the form of another new male client. On the phone he described his house as 'the last before the forest'. To help me find it he would meet me in the country town, outside the post office. He would be on his motorbike and I could follow him home. A thought about bikers and bodies buried in forests did cross my mind, but I assumed life would look after me as usual, and agreed to go.

It was a sunny day, a pleasant enough drive and there at the post office was a helmeted man on a motorbike. We gestured to each other and he took off with me following. I still had not seen his face. From the tarmac we headed onto a long gravel road, between houses then farmlets. Finally we stopped, as he had said, at the edge of a forest. Hoping all would be well, I drove in and parked outside his modest house, noticing the trailers, old tyres, water tanks, and assorted debris all over his property. We were in a valley. On the other side of the house were fruit trees and a field with a few cattle and trees, stretching into a long and beautiful bucolic view.

He climbed off his bike, removed his helmet, shook my hand and thanked me for coming. My fears had been totally unjustified. I was to spend the day with one of the gentlest, humblest, most sensitive souls I have ever had the pleasure of meeting.

As he showed me around the property, which used to belong to his parents, he pointed sadly to the cattle and said he hadn't eaten meat for a long time now.

"Why is that?" I asked.

"Well," he replied, "I used to ask them which one of them would like to sacrifice itself for me, and one of them would always step forward. Lately, none of them are stepping forward."

His vegetable garden was quite close to the house. This was handy, because, he explained to me, at night he sometimes heard his cabbages screaming as the snails ate them. He would get up at all hours to rescue his tormented cabbages from this cruel fate. When he picked his vegetables he did it with the gratitude and respect of the Native Americans.

Being so aware had its problems: second-hand shops were too painful for him, as he heard the stories of each item and they all begged him to take them home. I had discovered through my work that there is indeed consciousness and story in everything, so I could believe him.

Whereas I used to tune in to these levels of sensitivity for my work, it seemed he was permanently tuned in at a higher level of acuity. Happy to have a slightly kindred spirit there who would listen, he enthusiastically led me up the road into the forest to see if I could feel the strange parallel lines of energy he felt there. My lack of acuity here was probably a bit of a disappointment.

This sensitive man was currently working as a car mechanic, and felt like a square peg in a round hole. His cherished dream was to be a long-range weather forecaster, using a complex system he had worked out. I was presented with a list of forecasts to check for accuracy as time passed. Unfortunately the accuracy turned out to be not too high, but then the Bureau of Meteorology has been known to fail too.

Last time I visited this gentle man he was keenly studying natural health, and his house was as chaotic as ever. He had bored for water where my dowsing had suggested, and found it; and I was relieved to hear he had been eating meat again.

Driving home I pondered on the easy acceptance our society offers those who fit the norm – yet those a little different, with their unique offerings, so often struggle to find belonging. Through barriers of thoughtless prejudice, our society impoverishes not only them, but itself. How much we might all stand to gain by a warmer welcome of these unusual peoples' perception and participation.

On immigrating to Australia from apartheid South Africa I had expected to possibly be the recipient of some abuse due to the racist policies of my homeland. Anti-apartheid protests were happening in many parts of the world at the time. Instead I was pleasantly surprised to encounter a warm welcome generally.

A similar pleasant surprise greeted me on changing from health professional to feng shui consultant. I consulted in all sorts of business premises and would have expected to encounter more scepticism than I did. I was aware of how odd I must have looked standing there with eyes closed, or walking following a piece of bent wire, but employees seemed more interested than anything else.

Only once did I encounter some resistance, in a car mechanic's workshop. One of the mechanics came up to me and said, "I believe in Jesus", in other words, 'not this hocus pocus'. I confess I asked him if he still brushed his teeth, in other words: 'no matter what we believe we still need to attend to certain things ourselves.'

I Turn Magician and the Wine-Loving Naturopath

There were the mysterious feng shui cases and there were increasingly inexplicable events in my personal life too. Our wise teacher had told us that in practising feng shui we would be speeding up our spiritual development. That does make sense. Feng shui, like the martial arts and traditional Chinese medicine, is based on energy and how it interacts with matter. In working with energy one is closer to the heart of reality than when working with matter, which, it turns out is all energy anyway. Einstein had figured that out.

Feng shui recognises and utilizes the interconnection of space, direction, time, elements and people. We learnt about earth energies and lines of consciousness and how to map them on a floor plan using dowsing. We were given colour coding – brown for fault lines, blue for underground water and so on. On one of my early jobs I was mapping these lines and had forgotten which colour to use for leylines. I thoughtfully traced the position of the line on the floor plan with my finger while trying to remember. To my utter astonishment a green line appeared on the map where I had traced it with my finger! And of course green was the correct colour for leylines.

In my spare time I was dipping into various kinds of meditation apart from transcendental. I tasted Buddhist, Zen and Tibetan varieties and made up my own. I underwent a Taoist initiation with a master and experimented with all sorts of energy work, using methods from Barbara Anne Brennan to Donna

Eden, and making up many of my own techniques. I discovered kinesiology and qi gong, and the use of colour and sound in healing. The mind-body-etheric connection was becoming known and I found it fascinating.

One of my early clients was a local yoga teacher and I attended her classes. During the first class I was surprised to psychically see an Indian yogi all dressed in white standing near me. I felt that was enough reason to continue.

If I was off colour I went to a most unusual naturopath by the name of Ladislav Idrizovic, who would sometimes offer me a glass of red wine while he drank one himself. He either joked or grumbled while he diagnosed and treated me with brilliance, precision and frequencies, via all sorts of sophisticated machines. I recall him once correcting the twelfth level of my energy field. Planets came into it too. He had a dedicated following of people whose minds were open to alternatives or complements to the allopathic medical model, many of whom had been failed by that model. I knew that if I couldn't free myself of some energy I had picked up from work, I could rely on Ladi to do so.

Cosmic Visitations and Telepathic Dictation

'One thing I have learned in a long life: that all our science, measured against reality, is primitive and childlike... It is entirely possible that behind the perception of our senses, worlds are hidden of which we are unaware.'

– Albert Einstein

Many unexpected things happened in 1996. One evening after turning on the TV, I stepped back and apologized as I felt sure I had stepped on someone's toes. But I was alone in the house. When Ray was called to come and investigate, he told me there were two extraterrestrials in my home who had come for a reason, and they would be with me for a while.

I had built a deck at the front of my house and from there had a view down over Melbourne city and a glimpse of the distant bay. Soon after that, for many nights in a row, I stood on my deck watching what could only have been UFOs, (more recently known as UAPs), cavorting over Melbourne and the bay. A larger red light hung stationary in the sky with smaller ones coming and going from it. Their movement would at times be sudden and impossible for normal aircraft. Many people reported such UFO activity over Melbourne at around the same time.

One night the same year, a flattened line appeared across my back lawn. It shone silver in the moonlight and lasted unchanged for weeks, despite mowing. I had no idea how it had been made but received a strong intuitive warning not to go to that part of the garden for a while. There were strange smells in the night, of burning or chemicals; some of the plants at the back were burnt and my dogs were behaving oddly, sniffing all around the garden and appearing afraid.

Driving near my home I was surprised when a black stone came hurtling out of the sky onto the car bonnet. Its trajectory was straight down. I had no explanation. There were no tall buildings in the area. When this happened again in a different place about a week later, I stopped and retrieved the stone. It had fallen with such force that it had penetrated all the paint layers on the car bonnet and laid bare the metal, causing a small dent. The stone itself was surprisingly light, considering the damage it had done. Completely puzzled by this double occurrence, I looked up 'black stones from the sky' on Google, and found this is how the black Kaaba stone worshiped at Mecca had first appeared. One site told me that the recipients of these black stones, probably meteorites, are thought to be messengers: people who will deliver a message to humanity.

By then I had been writing intuitively, or 'channeling' as I called it, for a couple of years. I had received guidance from a range of different beings and was less concerned about who they were than about the accuracy of their messages. However I was rather taken aback when I was asked by a group of Pleiadians called The Others, to write a book for them. They told me it would be telepathically dictated and I just needed to trust them and listen. So that is what I did.

It was awe-inspiring as they told me much I did not know, which has later proved to be true. It was also very moving for me as I felt their depth of care for humanity and their sense of urgency. They seemed so much wiser and more visionary than us. Their concern was that we need to wake up to the futures we are creating for ourselves and our planet. They made it clear that many others in the cosmos are affected by our actions, and that we have the power to create a more favourable future by becoming more conscious. It was also emphasized that we are in a time of great change for our planet and all on it, and that our choices will determine how successful that change will be for all concerned.

Signals into Space

We send signals into space
Hoping one day for an answer
We think maybe our race
Is not the only dancer

But what if countless others
Have watched us all along
Regarding us as brothers
Without echoing our song

We assume we are the only type
That feels and thinks and talks
We are so full of certain hype
That nature surely balks

But what if that is arrogance
And nature's just like us
With sensitive intelligence
We throw under the bus

This planet is for us we say
We cut and drill and burn
Not thinking of another day
Of our grandchildren's turn

But what if it was never ours
And we are part of it
Put here to employ our powers
To nurture every bit

Surely it is high time now
To open sleepy eyes
To slay our faulty holy cows
And consider getting wise

A Soapbox, a Melted Mattress and a Disconcerting Theory

Filled with the Pleiadians' sense of urgency, I typed their book, made some copies and stood on my soapbox at a Mind Body Spirit Festival, giving away $10 copies and telling all who would listen. I wrote a synopsis and sent it off to a publisher, who showed an immediate interest. It was not long before I intuited a 'No no!' feeling and stopped the process. A similar thing happened a year later. Again the 'No no!' and I pulled it back.

Meanwhile strange things continued to happen. Each time I meditated, lying on my bed, I would be inundated with a powerful light almost instantly. This went on for about a week, after which the new mattress I had been lying on seemed damaged. The springs sagged. Had the power of this light melted them?

I had told a friend and client of mine, Carol, about my strange mystical adventures and one day she told me there was someone I should meet. She arranged for me and the German mother of her friend to meet with her for dinner. Marta seemed to have had some experience about ETs and thought I must be a 'host'. This meant, she explained, there was an ET cohabiting my body and influencing me strongly. She told me there was much to be gained from this, 'if they don't drive you mad first.'

This was rather disconcerting and I had no way to prove or disprove it. I may never know if Marta was right. One consolation about the mad bit was that having worked in acute psychiatric settings for so many years, I had a good idea what was insane and what wasn't, and could fairly confidently place myself in the latter category.

The Man who Lost Everything, the Green Passenger and the Wily Fox

Quite early in my new career I received a call from a somewhat distraught man in a country area. Bert told me that since he had moved to his current home, he had lost everything – his job, his wife, his money, his hair and even his teeth! As I climbed into my car I was hoping I knew enough to help this bereft man.

Then with my psychic vision I noticed something decidedly odd in the passenger seat. There sat a lanky, thin green ET! His arms and legs were rather like floppy green tubes, and as we drove on he looked like a child enjoying his very first car ride. Staring out of the window he appeared utterly enchanted, swinging his legs. By this time I was used to surprising anomalies in my strange life, so I took no notice. I thought perhaps this being had come to help in some way, but neither of us had any inclination to speak.

Leaving suburbia behind I drove into rolling hills, and on finding Bert's address, found myself driving along a thin ridge towards the house, which was perched atop a hill. The land fell away from the road all along the ridge, and then did the same around the hilltop house. A wonderful view, but absolutely no energy containment. I was relieved at the obviousness of the poor man's problem. Little energy even reached this house due to the thin ridge, and that would have simply blown away with the breeze, leaving him with no support at all.

Where energy flows away, so does good fortune. In this case the energy had dragged down the hill with it Bert's job, wife, money, hair and teeth. He had planted a tree or two, but it was not nearly enough to create a backdrop which would provide containment. Having explained the problem and delivered a few ideas, I did not need to linger long there. I never saw my green passenger again. Perhaps he had come to stay with Bert?

I once had a mini-version of this energy draining problem in my garden. My vegetable patch along the back fence suddenly seemed to be in very bad shape, with diseases abounding. I couldn't work out what was wrong for a while, then noticed a small burrow under the fence. Almost as soon as I closed up this hole, the plants' health improved! I had spread chicken manure, which had attracted a fox. He had dug his way in and wrecked the energy containment of the seven meter long garden, just by his small tunnel! These phenomena are still a source of amazement to me.

CHAPTER 6

Initiations, Miracles and Time Warps

An Aboriginal Initiation on Mount Warning

Feeling somewhat confused and a little embarrassed about the Pleiadian book, I shelved it for the time being and went off to visit my friend, Barbara in the rainforest of Queensland. She told me about Mount Warning, a sacred Aboriginal site where bush turkeys roamed, not far from where she lived. I was keen to climb it, so in the morning she and I and a couple of others drove to the start of the circuitous walk.

I lagged behind my friends as I started to psychically see the past being enacted on the lower slopes. There were Aboriginal people of past times, among the trees, scantily clad, fishing with spears, talking, playing and generally busy with their affairs. I was fascinated but, aware the others had gone ahead, turned away and slowly started to make my way up the winding path.

Then, to my left, about 2 meters into the bush, walking parallel to me, I saw with my psychic vision, a tall perfectly built young Aboriginal male, wearing only a loincloth and carrying a spear. When I mentally asked him why he was *walking with me, he replied that he had been appointed to accompany me to the top. So we continued walking in silence, with my friends now out of view, around a few corners.*

Reaching the top of Mount Warning entails using chains to climb over the last steep rocks. When I had scrambled up, there was my Aboriginal guide, pointing with his spear towards one of the viewing areas – the closest one on the left. He was instructing me to walk that way. My friends must have gone to one of the further areas. So I went to where he pointed and was immediately surrounded by Aboriginal men with white painted lines on their faces, who danced around me in a rhythmic circle with bent legs and stamping feet. By now I was so used to strange things happening to me that I took it in my stride and simply stood there until they were done, feeling honoured, grateful and puzzled about what it all meant.

It seemed to be some kind of initiation ceremony or healing. It felt so sacred that for many years I spoke of it to no-one. When I joined my friends they must have thought I had been dawdling.

A White Ghost from the Future

It is always reassuring to get some material corroboration of one's psychic perceptions. I wondered if there was some way I could find out if the Aboriginal men of that area did indeed paint white lines on their faces as I had seen psychically.

The next day this question was answered, when Barbara took me to a cultural centre at a place where young male initiation ceremonies used to be held. Outside this centre was a huge billboard and on it an illustration of Aboriginal men with exactly those white markings on their faces. We walked inside, though the building and into the land where the initiations had taken place.

One round grassed area felt terrible to me, so we walked on to a wetland where I again saw the past. Young men were climbing in the tree branches overhanging the water, jumping in and having a wonderful time. I told Barbara what I could see and she was intrigued and asked me to ask them some questions. I obligingly started a question and answer session with the boys until I saw behind us, in the distance, a tall Aboriginal man with a spear, standing on one leg, the other tucked up against his knee. He was watching us and looked concerned. Calling to the boys to stop talking to us, he started to walk towards us, at which point I told Barbara we had better move on.

Later I realized that to him we must have seemed like white ghosts from the future.

Healing Helpers and a Severed Head

At this stage I was not only doing feng shui consultations, but spiritual healings. After the Mount Warning initiation my healing ability became more powerful and effective. Beings from other dimensions would regularly come to help, sometimes seen by my clients but more usually by me. It often turned out that the beings who appeared held special meaning for the particular client. On one occasion I saw cherubs surround the client, and she was most moved by this as she had always been drawn to cherubs. Ascended Masters also came, including Jesus, and sometimes angels appeared. A client with a holocaust family history felt an angel around her and was greatly comforted to find that she was never alone, as she assumed she had been.

I found often the most successful sessions were those in which I took a passive role, being doorkeeper and interpreter, but leaving the healing action to the other beings. Often the client was moved by feeling the extent of the love felt towards him by the beings who had come to assist. I was usually given information to pass on, which helped in terms of insight, explanation or encouragement. One young woman told me she had lost her faith in life after her daughter's best friend had suicided. During the session her energy was worked on and pertinent information was passed on. Later, positively sparkling, she told me that her faith in life had been restored.

Two women came to me with brain tumours at around the same time. One dreaded the coming century, with its computers and technology. The other had recently bought a farm and was enthusiastically creating a beautiful garden and decorating her new home. The first felt little reason to carry on living, and died fairly soon after, while the second enjoyed many more years of life on her lovely farm, which I was lucky enough to visit later.

We delved at times into past lives and some intriguing things happened. One client who was a naturopath and friend came for a healing, and on tuning in I quickly saw a past life in which she had been beheaded in an execution. Etherically her head was sewn back on and, although the neck had not been the presenting problem, she reported how much more comfortable her neck felt from then on.

Although I had completed courses in Reiki and Chironic healing, I used neither method. It was more a case of inviting in helpful beings, particularly the Brotherhood of Light – a group of ascended masters – and then tuning in deeply. My psychic abilities, and my background in psychiatry and health sciences were invaluable. I was sometimes shown scenes from the person's childhood which had contributed to the current problem, and I found these could actually be changed, affecting the present. Understanding the root of the problems was very elucidating for the clients. Counselling for the present situation was often given, which complemented the energy work.

As time went on I took a more and more passive role – merely inviting the beings in, then looking, listening and reporting. When problems were psychological they were more easily healed. Once solidified into bodily ailments, I learnt not to expect as much instant change.

Breathy Turtles and Tricks of Time

A few months after the Mount Warning incident, I visited Barbara again and we took her kayak further north and into the sea, looking for dugongs. I found I could sense where they were and communicate with them. Soon we had a gang of giant turtles breathing noisily around us, their dignified gnarled heads above water, while dugongs swam beneath us. It was unforgettable and we felt awestruck and honoured to be in their company.

My channeling continued, and in 1998 whoever it was seemed to be trying to teach me about the vagaries of time and how to stretch time. I could not seem to understand it. Nonetheless, when a friend and I went to the art gallery one day we were amazed to find we had somehow gained an hour, according to both our watches!

In 2005 I consulted my channeling about a strange case:

> I worked today at a function centre, where a couple had got married. Tragically, 8 days after the wedding, the new husband was killed by the recent tsunami in Thailand. The business of the function centre, in Melbourne, suddenly went downhill after the tsunami. When I tuned into the energy of the centre I saw a sort of time tube - with the bride's anxiety (at the wedding) ricocheting back between the past and the future. The center had been part of

this scene, so much of the anxiety was being deposited there. Can you tell me more about this?

The tube of time you saw was right. That bride had had a sense of doom around the wedding. Part of her had been centred in the future, and knew what was to come. That part of her was not conscious. When the tsunami struck, that future memory, still in the function center, was activated by the strength of the present happening. In the man-made linear tube of time the past and present caught up with each other in a huge explosion of fear, grief and knowing. These feelings were breathed in by the function center and tainted it.

Once that traumatic energy was cleared from the function centre, all went well again… until the next time! The owners of the function centre were regular clients, as the centre was situated in a treed public park which seemed to attract drug users. There were negative entities and several attempted robberies, which left their mark energetically. Although weddings generally left happy energy in their wake, funerals often did not. So this was another reason for my visits.

Time

It seems that I grew up sometime
And had some parents dear,
But they are to be seen no more
So were they ever here?

It seems I lived in many homes
Both far away and near,
But now I do not dwell in them
So were they really there?

I know too well that now exists
Because right now I'm here,
But where has all the past gone
And was it ever there?

Could the past idea be just
A story from somewhere -
Something I dream up right now
That was not ever there?

And what about the time to come -
The future as we say.
Does that in fact exist at all
Or just dissolve away?

Is there a future we can reach
Or just another now,
A pile of nows with nothing else -
A river called the Tao?

Could it be that this is it:
That this is how we're set?
That now is not a bridge between
But all we ever get?

That now is where the power lies
And where the motivation;
And now the only time there is
For our life's creation.

Oh No! The Broken Leg and the Tragic Trip

Every now and then the results of a feng shui consultation did not go according to plan.

After one such visit Aishah was hanging up a crystal as prescribed, when she fell off the chair and broke her leg. I was mortified. That wasn't supposed to happen! However it was in fact just what the doctor had ordered.

Aishah later reported that during her long spell in bed she had time to ponder on her life and career. She realized she hated her job and had options. This resulted in her resigning and starting a new career in journalism, which she loved. She told me the broken leg had been a blessing.

Another client reported after having her house 'done', that her daughter had had a serious car accident. There was much damage, but Iris was fine, luckily. I felt concerned that this shouldn't happen after feng shui, but the very positive mother was sure something good would come of it.

What happened was that Iris owed so much money for the car repairs, she traded in the ticket her parents had bought her to go overseas for her 21st birthday present. She had been booked to go on a certain adventure trip, in which many young people subsequently lost their lives. Her mother later told me the family believe the feng shui may well have saved Iris's life.

Life takes its own twists and turns, and is a mystery. A single guiding intelligence runs through it all that we cannot possibly fathom.

The impossible continued to disprove itself in so many ways in my strange life. I never knew when some odd thing would happen which seemed to break all the normal rules of life.

Marvelous Miracles – Ducks, Dollars and a Gold Star

One day I did a healing on two of my closest friends. The following day two shrubs which had finished blooming, and which I had been meaning to prune back, suddenly had new red flowers all over them. This defied all the laws of nature. There had been deadheads all over and no new buds. The shrubs had gone from brown to red overnight.

Soon after that, I had a vision of the untidy bushes at the end of the court being trimmed into neat squares, and later that day they were, with a chainsaw. Had I switched time tracks into the future for a minute?

One morning after walking my dogs in a local park, with its creek and ducks, I had a fleeting thought that it would be lovely to have ducks in my garden. On arriving home I was delighted to find two ducks perkily queuing up at my gate to be let in! I filled a bath of water for them and enjoyed their visit, with the dogs safely in the house.

I often drove to clients in the country. After one such job, driving home quite late, I was hungry and had a brief fantasy about buying a pizza, before deciding I would rather have something healthier at home. Walking up my garden path I was puzzled to see something triangular on my lawn. It was a large cheesy slice of pizza! Something or someone had heard my fleeting request. Needless to say it was upside down and I did not eat it.

On another occasion I was busy at a client's house, out the back taking a compass reading, when I saw a $20 note on the ground. I picked it up, passed it to Heather and told her where I'd found it, near the washing line.

"Oh," she said, "Thanks, it must have fallen out of a pocket."

We thought no more about it until it was time for me to leave and we were walking down her drive towards the gate. Banknotes kept appearing in front of me on the ground. As they appeared I picked them up and gave them to Heather. In the end they possibly paid for the consultation. Goodness knows how or even why that happened. I had had no fleeting thought about creating money! Maybe Heather had…

Then there was a very important consultation. It was the principal's house at a prestigious boys' school. I was well aware that many boys who would later be in influential positions would attend this school, so the feng shui of this house could have far reaching ramifications. I did my best, cleared the energy, made recommendations and wrote my report.

While the principal's wife went to the bank for funds to pay me, I waited outside in the garden and silently prayed I had done the job well enough. When I opened my eyes and looked down, my prayer was answered by the presence of a metal gold star at my feet! When my client returned I showed it to her, asking if she had seen it before. She had not. I don't know why I gave it to her – it would have been such a nice memento.

For many years I regarded these events as miracles. Now I realize most, if not all, were simply manifestations as a result of thoughts. We are very powerful beings. However some of these events had nothing to do with my thoughts at the time, for instance the shrubs re-flowering and the bank notes appearing. Maybe these happened purely to show me that anything is possible, or that the material world is more malleable and unreal than we take it to be.

Another interesting incident demonstrating our power happened one night on my way home in the country. My car was old, and the heat gauge on the dashboard was rising. The engine water had run low and boiled before. Now I watched in dismay as the warning dial went from green to orange to red. What to do? I was on a country road nowhere near a garage.

So I decided I must surely be able to cool it down with my mind. I imagined cool water pouring in, and to my relief and surprise the dial went back to orange then green. That night I arrived home safely. Did the power of my mind save the day, or did I receive help from other beings or life itself? Is there any difference between me and life itself? Was it Life helping life?

Magic

There is magic in this place
Feel it surge through your humming veins.
The light plays music in your eyes
And your mind stretches to forever.
There is magic here -
A dancing in your footstep,
And colour in the air.
Here the Earth has union with the Heavens
And all is well.

Initiations from a Native American and a Crow

The psychic phenomena continued.

One night, awake in bed, I found myself sitting on the ground in front of a fire with an imposing native American chief. He ceremoniously handed me the peace pipe, which we smoked together in silence. This was happening when I lay in bed on my left. When I turned onto my right I was looking down the dry valley at the encampment of teepees stretching into the distance, woodsmoke curling above them. I was aware of being there at the same time as I was in bed, and the change of scene whenever I turned was intriguing. This seemed to be another initiation.

I think the first of these strange initiations had been given to me by a crow, on a mountain top in Australia many years before this. A friend and I had climbed up to the top of Mount Buffalo and were admiring the view, when a crow landed in front of us on the stone parapet. He hopped directly in front of me and proceeded to address me. It was not a song. It was a speech. Unfortunately as I do not speak Crow I will never know what he said, but he certainly meant it. He addressed me for some time, looking me straight in the eye. To me it represented something about our connection with the other species. He certainly felt a connection and seemed to expect me to as well.

Years later, I came upon a butterfly who understood this connection.

Butterfly Gratitude

Driving to a country job
A place I had not been
I saw a coloured flapping blob
Stuck to the windy screen

Pulling over to the side
The flapping became still
She'd had a horror ride and
Poor butterfly looked ill

Orange, black and white was there
She still had so much beauty
But one wing had a tear
And I took it as my duty

To place her on the other seat
Her tiny heart a-throb
She sat there quiet and neat
As we drove on to my job

Afterwards I drove her home
And placed her in my flowers
I left her free to roam
To heal in sunny hours

In about a week or so
While lunching on my deck
I watched my garden grow
Then I saw a flying speck

Round and round my head it flew
Then landed on my plate
Orange, black and white the hue
It was my little mate.

Slowly as if to make a point
She flapped open her wings
To show that tear still there
And her gratitude still sings

Hungry Rats and Mischievous Possums

The connection with nature came in useful in some feng shui consultations. On a visit to my parents in South Africa, my brother, a professor at the University of Cape Town, kindly arranged for me to give a talk on feng shui at the university. Feng shui was almost unknown in South Africa at the time, and the hall was packed with people eager to learn about it. After the talk several members of the audience sought my services, and the consultations that followed paid for my trip. I consulted to a horse stud, a hairdresser, a kindergarten, several houses and a restaurant.

The restaurant was having trouble with rats. They had tried everything but nothing deterred the hungry rodent trespassers. Finding no obvious feng shui problem, I decided to talk to the rats directly. Intuitively I asked telepathically to speak with the head rat. I explained to him the dilemma he and his minions were causing to the restaurateur, and asked if he could make some sort of compromise. A deal was reached. The restaurant staff would regularly put out some bread in an adjacent empty lot, and the rats would leave the restaurant alone. To my delight, and the client's, this worked a charm – no more rats in the restaurant!

A friend of mine told me her mother was a keen rose grower but was going crazy as the possums kept eating her flowers. When I tuned in to the head possum to have a little talk about this situation, I almost heard guffaws. Apparently the possums were enjoying not only the roses, but much amusement from the old lady's frustration! I sternly told the boss possum that it was no laughing matter for the old lady, whose hobby this was.

Eventually he agreed to a deal. Once a week an apple was to be put in the garden for the possums, in exchange for non-interference in the rose beds. This seemed fair. I also suggested to the lady that should the possums break the deal, she not give them the satisfaction of showing any frustration. This seemed to work and my friend soon reported that her mother was enjoying her roses again.

CHAPTER 7

Pure Energy and Tantalizing Travels

Pan and the Gift of Changing Places

Fairly soon after I started feng shui, Pan came to me as I was sitting in my lounge. Again, it was my psychic vision that enabled me to see him. He told me to always first connect with him when I work. Later, when those supposed miracles occurred, I did wonder if they were his doing. But by then I had helped numerous earthbound souls, had worked with angels and had connected with nature spirits, as well as extraterrestrials, so I had little idea about who was responsible for what in my peculiar life.

Perhaps due to those initiations, or due to my relationship with Pan, I was blessed to have gifts that most feng shui consultants did not have. Initially I had used mudras and mantras taught by the qi gong master to clear the energy of places, but soon I found I was able to clear the energy of places and items with my mind. Gradually my technique became very simple.

I realized, through my meditations, that underlying all manifestation was a field of perfect unsullied purity. I found I could destroy unfortunate memories and thought forms in places safely and effectively just by tuning in to this inherent perfection.

This original unspoilt field of energy is stronger than any overlay which has occurred since, and can never be changed. When a place is reminded of its primary truth, the untruth simply dissolves. Clients would often feel the difference immediately or see it as being lighter. Often as the energy cleared, the sun would come out from a cloud, or a bird would sing. Friends of clients on more than one occasion later remarked that they liked the new paint of the room, when it had not been painted!

Places get conned by illusion, just as people do. This phenomenon gave me cause to ponder about our punitive 'justice' systems, and how much more effective it might be to somehow show criminals their inherent goodness, rather than focussing on mistakes made.

One day, early in my energy-clearing days I was in awe, when I closed my eyes and tuned in, to clearly see the war in the heavens. I had vaguely heard this term before and imagined this to be a myth, but there it was playing out above me, visible via my third eye. It was a mighty scene of angelic battle and I have no idea why it was shown to me. Perhaps it was a case of like attracts like, as I did at that stage rather regard myself as some kind of spiritual warrior working for the light against the dark. As my understanding progressed with time, that view changed to a more harmonious, less polarised one.

Beyond thought

Out beyond
Beyond the turgid
Caverns of obsessive thought
Beyond regurgitated history
Is a crystal place
Pristine and shining
Fresh birthplace of Now
Effervescing fountain
Of eternal creation
Infinite dynamic
Empty space.

It was not only places that I found myself clearing. Dr Maseru Fmoto had conducted experiments with water crystals demonstrating that water holds memories, and is affected by speech, prayer and emotion. In my experience, all matter can hold memories. I found myself clearing the memories in the energy fields of all sorts of things, which were affecting their owners.

The Gangster's Car, The Conflicted Cruet Set and the Furious Toaster

I had been to the prestige car dealer before and he had been happy with the result. Some months later he phoned me to tell me about all manner of new problems he was having with the business. During my subsequent visit all appeared well initially. When I tuned in however, I felt a very nasty energy and my dowsing rod led me to a fancy red sports car. I told Dimitri the energy of that car was his problem. He and his secretary passed each other an odd secretive look. After I had cleared the energy of that car all again went well for Dimitri's business.

I later found out that that car had belonged to a well-known criminal gangster, often seen on the news for the gang warfare and murders he was embroiled in.

I had to clear the energy of many cars. One was upset that its long-time owner had been talking of selling it. Another had been involved in a crash, and carrying 'crash-energy', was attracting more of them. A truck with particularly horrible energy had witnessed a paedophile's action in it.

One family who were generally happy together, reported that they always fought at the dinner table and they could not work out why. It was uncharacteristic. I checked out the room. It was OK. I checked out the table. It was also OK. Then my dowsing rod pointed me to the innocent-looking cruet set, always kept on the table. On tuning in to it I felt the unpleasant conflict of previous owners. My client then told me she had bought it at an opportunity shop – it was second hand and had obviously taken on conflict energy from the past. After the discordant memory was removed, dinners for that family became as harmonious as they should have been all along.

Perhaps the strangest item I ever had to clear was a toaster. I had been to Margie's home and business many times over the years. This time in discussing various things, she happened to mention that they had a brand new toaster, but to their annoyance it always burnt the toast. I walked over to it and had a look. Sparkly and new-looking, it was one of those wide-mouthed toasters which could accommodate crumpets as well as bread. When I tuned in and asked it why it always burnt the toast, I was astonished to find it having a tantrum. If it could have, it would have stamped its feet!

"I am special!" It was shouting, "I am made for crumpets, not just for toast!"

I could not help laughing, even though the toaster obviously felt this was no laughing matter. I instructed Margie to make sure they regularly used it for crumpets. They religiously did so, then when they made toast, it was no longer burnt. In writing this I am contemplating on the fact that the element the toaster uses to perform its job is electricity – fire. Maybe that accounted for its fiery temperament!

Sometimes I had to clear the energy of the walls of a house. The building material, rather than the space between, was the problem. In these cases there had often been conflict in the building process, between workers involved. Or the energetic problem could even have come about during the manufacturing process. If plasterboard, or any other building material, is made in an environment of negative energy, the product will likely imbibe that energy and carry it to where it is used. This should come as no surprise, considering how our own childhoods affect our future lives, and how dogs mistreated early on may well bite later.

Human consciousness and vibration have a strong effect on much-used items. I found rings often held the emotional and health history of their owners within them. Items such as this can greatly affect future wearers, for good or ill.

You may have heard it said that if you treat your appliances with appreciation and respect, they will last longer. A friend of mine had an ancient car held together with tape. She called it Happiness, loved it dearly, talked to it, and it just kept on going for her. A young model client told me her husband, also a model, felt sorry for any of his clothes that were not worn. He would regularly revolve them in his cupboard, so all would have a turn to be worn and none would feel left out. There is an interesting book on a related topic, called *Behaving As If the God in All Life Matters*, by Machaelle Small Wright.

Very occasionally I came across items whose energy had been so altered, through and through, that they could not be cleared and had to be discarded. The underlying perfection was no longer there as the baseline, or maybe it was so overwhelmed as not to be contactable.

Working in acute psychiatry it had been very apparent to me that no matter what people had been through and no matter how they had reacted, there remained the light of goodness within them. I wondered if it was possible that in some other milieus people might be found whose inner light had been extinguished altogether, as in these items I could not clear. This might explain some of the worst psychopathic behaviour encountered.

All is light.

All else is illusion.

Bewitched Boats, Witch Doctors and an Elephant

Any idea of an anthropomorphic God, perched upon a throne up high, judging and sentencing mankind to heaven or eternal damnation had long been dissolved here. For one thing it made no sense. How could such a God be omnipresent? To be omnipresent would entail pervading all species including us, not being away in the sky.

I had delved a bit into quantum physics and ancient texts, and had had my own meditation experiences, which had convinced me that the omniscient, omnipresent, omnipotent organizing force of the universe was infinitely intelligent. The complex web of events and interactions woven was far beyond any mortal comprehension and also far beyond randomness. The statistical evidence that this whole show was not due to random evolution of atoms and molecules was beyond doubt. And what did this all mean in terms of how to live our lives? I wanted to understand more.

Shortly after I started my feng shui work, I was clearly told that I must go away and have a rest from it, at least four times per year. So I regularly went away for weekends and several times ventured overseas for longer holidays. Always on the lookout for clues about life and the truth of our existence, these holidays gave me glimpses I might not have had at home, as well as refreshment.

In 1998 I was reading the Sunday paper at my brother-in-law's house in Pretoria, South Africa, having visited my parents near Cape Town, when I saw a tempting advertisement. A two week tour of Zimbabwe, including Victoria Falls and a few days on a houseboat on Lake Kariba!

The Kariba Dam had been built between 1955 and 1959 on the Zambezi river, to provide hydroelectric power to both Northern and Southern Rhodesia (now Zambia and Zimbabwe). The largest man-made lake in the world, when Lake Kariba was formed, thousands of Tonga people living on both sides of the Zambezi were displaced and had to be resettled. The other major problem was wildlife, as the waters of the dam and lake rose. From 1958 to 1964 Operation Noah took place, capturing and rescuing thousands of large and small animals. Elephants, antelopes, rhinos, lions, leopards, zebras, warthogs, birds and snakes were rescued and released on the mainland or in national parks.

Of course I could not resist this trip, which was very reasonably priced in my Australian dollars. The first bit of this tour I remember was being in a train with the rest of the tour members, including our guide, Doris, who had led this trip umpteen times before. Doris was disconcerted that the train was not leaving when it normally did.

We sat in the stationary train for about nine hours, with Doris repeatedly declaring, "This has NEVER happened before."

I kept a bit quiet. Truth be known I had noticed I seemed to often have a strange effect on electrical or mechanical things. My computer at home would regularly behave in very uncomputerly ways, as would my watch. (This strange problem struck again later in 2008. I was in the dentists' chair, about to have my amalgams replaced, when to the consternation of the poor dentist, the power of the whole dental practice went down!)

Eventually the train started and off we went. It was a marvelous holiday, staying in whitewashed, thatched riverside lodges with warthogs running across lawns and outdoor sunset banquets. We walked past steaming elephant dung to witness the awe-inspiring spectacle of Victoria Falls at its rainbow-making best. I walked on the slippery, wet, narrow bridge across the top of it, from Zimbabwe to Zambia, the thunder and rainbow-spray overwhelming.

The days on the houseboat were wonderful too. This large boat contained several little boats that we could take in pairs to go close to the shore and watch the animals, many of which came to bathe or drink. Here my dark secret was revealed!

By this time most of the others knew that I was some kind of weird witch – working with energy and ghosts. After each boat I ventured into either got a broken rudder or some other mechanical ailment that needed rescue, no-one was game to pair with me! It became something of a joke.

However I still got to go up close and personal with elephants, hippos and many other beautiful animals. In fact, first with an elephant then with a lion, there was prolonged eye contact, and a profound sense of connection and energy exchange. I felt some of the patient solid elephant energy entering me, and from the lion, a sense of strength and courage. Goodness only knows what they received from me!

We had some time off from the group, during which I arranged for a local driver to take me to a real witch doctor, now called a sangoma. This man was one who worked with the local people and was not involved in tourism. I was driven way into the bush, and eventually to a dusty property containing a small hut. What impressed me at once was the young woman standing in the grounds. She was statuesque and healthy-looking in a way seldom seen. The word 'sovereignty' sprang to mind. If she was the witch doctor's daughter this boded well.

In the little hut there was the usual leopard skin, bones and other witch doctor accoutrements, and the witch doctor of many dreadlocks soon put himself into a trance. Fortunately there was an interpreter who told me several things I must do, including to put a coin on the floor of the houseboat where two paths crossed. I don't recall this session having any noticeable effect upon me, but maybe it woke some ancestors up to my existence and needs.

Then we were off to the Zimbabwe Ruins, which I had heard of but never seen. Known too as Great Zimbabwe, these ruins are a Unesco World Heritage site. Great Zimbabwe was a medieval African city – part of a wealthy African trading empire that controlled much of the East African coast from the 11th to the 15th centuries. However, the city was largely abandoned by the 15th century as the Shona people migrated elsewhere, for reasons still not understood.

The ruins of the city are now a popular tourist site and here we explored some fascinating structures, including the top of the rocky hill where we were told the preacher would stand to address the people.

Then, of course, I visited the resident tourist witch doctor who, on discovering I too was a healer, was all for taking me out into the bush the following day to gather medicinal herbs to take back to Australia. Sadly we were leaving the following day, besides the Australian Border Force would not have taken kindly to the idea of unknown African herbs invading our land.

I fell in love with Zimbabwe on that trip and still have many beautifully crafted stone and wood carvings, including two big rather imposing wooden Zimbabwe birds. These birds, possibly representing the fish eagle, are the Zimbabwean national emblem, seen on its flag, coat of arms and money.

Coke Bottles, a Pleiadian Festival and Lake Titicaca

In mid 2000 I joined an adventure tour to Peru and Bolivia. I had had the words 'Lake Titicaca' appear in my head in the night some time before and was intrigued, as it is reputed to be a powerful sacred site. This three week trip included a nine day trek through the Andes culminating in the Inca Trail to Machu Picchu, another beautiful and sacred site.

I trained by climbing local mountains with cans of beans in a backpack, and on Ladi's advice, I bought a kilogram of organic dried apricots to prevent altitude sickness. These apricots worked a treat and, unlike many, I had no problem. As soon as I felt short of oxygen I chewed one or two. Strangely, no-one took me up on my offer to share.

Having trekked for days in the barren Andes, hearing snow cracking off high mountains some minus 11 degree Celsius nights; and enjoying less and less oxygen, we felt utterly remote from civilization. Suddenly one day a group of women with their huge skirts and hats and bundled blankets appeared over the horizon. Where did they come from? To our amusement they set their bundles on the ground and opened them up to reveal cans of Coke and Fanta for sale! Civilization had found us – we were obviously not quite as remote as we had thought!

The lush Inca Trail was very different. I was impressed to see giant native versions of so many of the domesticated plants we have in our gardens.

Alstroemeria, fuschias, orchids, periwinkles – their colours dazzling among the bountiful greenery.

One rainy day our thoughtful and competent guide, a Peruvian man, offered us games and literature to keep us amused in our wet tents. I ran dripping to his tent and picked up a handful of articles to read. To my amazement, the literature I had unknowingly taken was about the Mayan connection to the Pleiades. I had channelled the Pleiadian book only a few years earlier. Apparently, historically the appearance of the Pleiades in the sky heralded the beginning of the growing season, and this day was still celebrated with a festival. As if that synchronicity wasn't enough, the date of this festival coincided with our short tour, and after our trek we watched the colourful, noisy celebration in a Peruvian town square. We were dazzled by wide-skirted dancers, marvelous hats and masks, panpipe and bamboo flute players, excited children ducking between adults, and woven cloths all the colours of the rainbow.

Then after enjoying the rich musical culture of Cusco, we were off to Lake Titicaca and onto floating islands made of reeds. The people living on these man-made islands have the benefit of not paying taxes. The men tend to take their reed boats to the mainland for work, while the women, many obese from lack of exercise, sell their crafts to tourists. To our surprise they all had television aerials, the televisions having been donated by a charity to help entertain them through the cold winter months.

'What a well-meaning but colonial attitude that was', we thought. How would bringing the consumer-oriented world with all its trinkets and toys into these peoples' lives have affected their children? How satisfied would they now be with their simple, natural lives when comparing them to the glitz of life on television? And how easy would it be for any of them to make the switch from one to the other in reality? Materially wealthy groups helping those less affluent is a delicate dance, with so many factors needing to be considered, not least respect of culture.

King Arthur and my Mother

The following year, on the advice of a client of mine, I took my daughter with me to the sacred sites of England and Wales. We walked up the mystical Glastonbury Tor; surveyed the ruins of Glastonbury Abbey, where I thought I saw angels; were surrounded by nature spirits in the charming garden at Chalice Well; admired Stonehenge and what remained of Woodhenge; wandered around King Arthur's Tintagel and bought a little bottle of holy water from Holywell in Wales.

Whether or not any benefit rubbed off on us from attending all these sacred sites, I may never know, but I like to think it did.

It was perhaps a less sacred part of that trip that was the most serendipitous. My mother had grown up in a charming little English village called Ledbury, in a large Tudor house called The Steppes with an adjoining thatched building called The Barn. We decided to go to Ledbury to see if we could find the old house.

It was unmissable, in its dark-beamed Tudor glory, on the main street, so we knocked on the door. We were greeted by the friendly owner who informed us that it was now a Bed and Breakfast. On hearing about my mother's history there, the owner kindly showed us around. She also showed us the brass plaque with the words 'Dr Tom Jones', that they had found in the garden. He had been my grandfather, the village doctor.

How could we resist? We spent the night in a pretty room upstairs, which we later found out from my mother had been her childhood bedroom!

A Barge Skipper, a Breatharian and More Tricks of Time

A couple of years later, in 2003, I spent a month in Sweden, with a friend, staying in a room in the garden of a Swedish friend of hers. They lived in a very picturesque spiritual community, of many red-roofed houses and a communal building surrounded by pretty gardens. Marianne was a psychologist and her partner Morgan was an interesting man who seemed spiritually advanced. He taught me that we have three brains – in the head, heart and gut.

While we were there, the idea of becoming a barge skipper took Morgan's fancy, and he started training for the job. This was lucky for us as we were invited to go on a barge trip down the wide canal, which changed height several times, requiring complicated maneuvers with locks. Along the banks we passed the full Swedish charm of people picnicking on green grass under shady trees.

I was amused to be instructed in the pragmatic Swedish adage: 'There is no bad weather, only unsuitable clothing.' Were that maxim applied indoors, even in sunny Australia, how much heating and cooling energy could be saved!

I loved the way the community lived – a relaxed friendliness pervaded and one often saw groups of men or women either working or chatting together. I gathered from Marianne that below this pleasant surface there was quite a shadow of mental illness among the Swedish people, not evident to a visitor like me.

The surrounding area was gently beautiful, with lakes, birches, wild flowers and fat white sheep. We gathered birch leaves from the forest, watching for bears, and made birch leaf cordial under Marianne's instruction. And we happened to be there at the right time of year to dance around the maypole with flower wreaths in our hair.

Living near this community was a young woman who made jewellery, rode her bicycle and never ate food. She had been a breatharian for many years, and had the most lustrous, velvety skin, which seemed to radiate energy in a way I had never seen before and have not seen since. I only saw her once but she left a big impression. Hers was the perfect life for breatharianism – fresh air, forests and working with jewels and metals.

I have heard of other breatharians who were tested by sceptical scientists. They were invariably shut in rooms with cameras, expected to prove they could manage to survive without food. Of course due to a lack of natural healthy energy, fresh air and sunlight to sustain them, most if not all, were doomed to fail, thereby only confirming the scepticism often underlying such experiments.

Vegans tend to believe they are being less cruel by not eating meat or dairy, but if what JC Bose (and many others since) discovered was correct, to avoid cruelty we might all need to become breatharians! Maybe a gentle alternative in the meantime is to kill, pick and eat with gratitude, as so many indigenous cultures did. Gratitude is a potent force which bounces back benefit to the person feeling it.

The time-honoured ritual of saying grace before a meal also possibly has the effect of reducing any residual trauma in our food, thus making it more nutritious.

Recent studies indicate that we can actually affect events that have already happened, by intentions held in the present. This would be explained by the idea that time only exists now – there is actually no linear time. For this reason, I like to bless the chickens that have contributed their necks to my dog's meals each day. I believe that blessing affects those farmed chickens while still alive.

While in Sweden, I was advised to catch a train up to the northern islands of Lofoten in Norway. My memory of this train trip consists of barren, grey-brown views of Lapland and flickering light, as we passed through endless mountain tunnels. Lofoten is exceedingly beautiful with its rugged mountains and fjords, and I spent one of the most enjoyable days of my life there on a hired bicycle.

I rode in and out of picturesque fishing villages, never knowing what beauty I would find around the next corner. One of the indelible scenes I was left with was of a woman walking towards me over a rise carrying a huge fish draped over her arms.

In this land of the midnight sun I rode until 11.30 p.m. in broad daylight and might not have stopped if I hadn't had to return the bicycle!

The Smile and The Terrified Burglar

Many of my trips away were to South Africa to visit my parents. On one such trip my mother suggested I visit Annika, an elderly friend of hers who had been a naturopath. Judging by a story Annika told me, she must have been spiritually wide awake.

South Africa has a shocking violent crime rate due to the large proportion of chronically disadvantaged people there. Burglaries often result in murders, so most houses are heavily fortified with burglar bars, alarms and all manner of protection.

Annika told me that one night she had heard a noise in the house. She had left her sleeping husband in bed and had walked towards the sound. In the dining room she saw a burglar climbing in through the window. When she simply stood still and smiled at him, apparently his expression turned to one of utter horror and he fled.

This reminded me of Christian advice to love our enemies. The dark cannot withstand the light, but few of us would dare to put that into practice the way Annika had. Being half-hearted about it might well have resulted in her murder. She must have been able to look beyond appearances at the intruder's soul, which was too much for him to bear.

CHAPTER 8

Ghosts and Dark Nights

Souls that go Bump In the Night

In between all these delightful travels I was earning my air tickets by my feng shui work. When clients had odd inexplicable things happening at home or work, I checked for the presence of ghosts, among other factors. I generally preferred to use the term 'earthbound spirits', as the word 'ghost' tends to be associated with fantasy or fear.

Occasionally souls revisit loved ones after bodily death and leave freely again, needing no help. But the ones stuck on the earth plane generally need help, and many of their disturbing actions can be to this end. In most cases I found it easy to help them on. Through mental communication and the aid of etheric beings, they could be shown that they were no longer in body and it was time to move on. A few had small requirements to be fulfilled before moving on. It may be hard to believe, but one actually believed he needed a packed lunch for the journey, so this was etherically given! When they were ready, usually instantly, angels would escort them.

Some, however, needed more help than that to clear layers of inner unfinished business, in the form of unresolved emotion. In these cases I would mentally step back and ask the angels to help them. Then I would watch and feel as they went through the layers of unresolved feeling, until they reached peace. When they finally left, there was always a wonderful expansive and light feeling. And my client was no longer bothered by strange happenings. In these cases I always felt my more valuable contribution was to the freed soul, rather than to the paying client.

I only ever came across one earthbound soul who had chosen not to leave due to having found his life so satisfying. He had been a doctor, and he too was eventually persuaded and helped to move on.

Occasionally I came across the earthbound souls of the original inhabitants of Australia. I felt it was not my place to send them on, instead stepping back and calling on their elders and ancestors from the Dreamtime to help, which they invariably did. I recall one place in which there seemed to be a sort of vortex filled with these stuck Aboriginal souls – probably a massacre site, of which there must be many. Their ancestors helped them on to a better phase of their journey.

Many of the popular stories told about dealing with earthbound spirits, in these cases invariably called 'ghosts', I found somewhat misguided. The idea of simply telling them to leave, throwing salt over your shoulder to protect yourself, lighting a candle, let alone the commercial 'ghost-busters', were of little help to these stuck souls. They were often treated as things to be got rid of or to be afraid of, rather than in fact lost people without bodies, needing assistance to find their way home. More needs to be understood about this phenomenon, so there can be more empathy and effective action for these souls.

The Photographer's Ghosts and the Anguished Parents

Some of the most moving experiences I had when consulting involved earthbound spirits. When the body has died, the soul or mind or identity can sometimes remain on this plane instead of moving on. There seem to be certain circumstances which cause this to happen. I came across spirits whose faculties were so confused either by dementia or drugs, that they did not know they had died. A similar thing can happen to those who die suddenly and unexpectedly. This was the case at a Malvern house I visited.

My client had had all sorts of strange things happening: doors opening, lights turning on or off and the TV sound changing. On tuning in there, I discovered the spirit of a young woman, who had come into the house for help, after being killed instantly in an accident on the busy road outside. It had been so sudden that she was not aware she had died.

With the right help, these souls can move on to wherever it is they belong. Often just seeing an angel on either side of them is enough for them to realize the situation and be escorted home. In most cases of earthbound spirits, however, I found that the person who has passed is kept back by compelling unfinished business.

When Jack called me, he seemed to have a string of problems, which he suspected were associated with the apartment in which he had his photography studio and lived with his family. I arrived in Duncan Street on a drizzly summer afternoon, and made my way into the large dark foyer of the probably once grand art deco building. After a moment of taking in the rather oppressive, dank and dusty feeling, I discovered the rickety lift with the old metal concertina door and, as Jack had instructed, landed on the first floor.

I rang the bell and was soon greeted by a smiling middle-aged man, who ushered me through a waiting room lined with large photographs and colourful couches. Unlike the building, Jack was warm, charming and friendly, and quickly made me feel at home. He showed me through the huge black painted spaces that served as his studio, which were empty but for collections of large lights and white reflective dishes. To one side, we checked out his smaller and much brighter offices.

Jack had the whole floor for work and home, and the home part was at the back. We chatted as we made our way towards the back, and Jack said, "Maybe you should see this too," as he opened the heavy door onto the metal fire escape. I instantly felt horribly sick and asked him to shut it again immediately, which he did.

Then we walked through a narrow passage lined with ribbons and a child's art, and a door opened into another world. Here was the apartment where Jack lived with his wife Alice, an ex-model 20 years his junior, and their three year old son Tom. Unlike the almost empty studio, the apartment was colourful and artistic, decorated with flair, originality and natural materials. The fact that they were a happy, harmonious little family was obvious, both from what Jack told me and from the look of their dwelling. But one of the reasons Jack had called me was that since Alice had told him of her pregnancy with Tom, he had suffered horrible nightmares. This made no sense to him, as he had been thrilled at the prospect of having a child, and adored Tom. He had also found himself being short-tempered with Alice, which was not his nature.

The other reasons for my visit were easily solved. Jack used to get up many times each night due, we found, to sleeping over an underground water stream; and Tom's health issues were due to the electromagnetic fields of cables behind his bed. But what of the nightmares and their strange timing?

So at this point I did my witchy thing and stood at the omphalos (the energy centre) of the building, with my eyes shut to tune in. The energy of the place did not feel clear. The next move was to use my dowsing rod, checking through a list of possible factors to identify what was affecting the energy field. I discovered there was not only a negative psychic impression, but also two earthbound spirits.

So my first job was to get rid of that entity. I asked the dowsing rod to lead me to it and it led me straight back to that fire escape door. This time I was not game to open it, but cleared the nauseating energy and dissolved the entity.

Then I asked the dowsing rod to take me to spirit number one. I was led into the huge dark studio, to a spot in the middle where I closed my eyes and tuned in. The spirit was a young man in soldier uniform and I asked him why he was still there.

He was apparently wracked with guilt and kept saying, "I didn't mean to – I was drunk… I didn't mean to… " His guilt was almost palpable and, like a thick rope of glue, was binding him to the floor. I felt immensely sorry for him, and did what I always did at times where the spirit needed healing. I stepped back literally and called in angelic beings to heal this young man's mind.

What might take a lifetime of psychotherapy could be achieved in a minute or two in this way. The spirit would rapidly pass through different stages: from guilt to grief to sorrow and eventually to peace, and once peace had been reached he would be ready, with help, to leave at last. It was always a very satisfying process and I judged this as probably the most important work I did.

So this young soldier left in peace, and I then followed my dowsing rod to find earthbound spirit number two. Once again I was led to the fire escape. On tuning in this time I saw a pathetic grief-stricken young woman. Then the whole scenario of what had happened there unfolded before me.

The woman was a poor prostitute who had no family, and had high hopes when she walked up the fire escape to tell the young soldier she was pregnant by him. She had been building castles in the air about a family at last, with respectability, affection and love. But when he opened the door to her he was drunk, and her excited words were met by a single push to her death down the metal fire escape.

After helping her on, I confess to being so overwhelmed by the sorrow of the whole event that I shed a little tear on Jack's empathic shoulder, as I told him this tragic story. He confirmed that during the second world war the building had been a soldiers' barracks. And the prostitution business of that area is well known and continues today. Jack then told me that this made sense of an apparition he had once seen in his bedroom while awake. He had seen a man and a woman arguing and a pool of blood on the floor. This also of course made sense of the nightmares he had had since hearing his wife was pregnant. Some part of his psyche had been picking up the consciousness of these two poor tortured souls.

Happily, after this visit, and a few simple changes, all was resolved. The health issues cleared up, Jack felt calmer and there were no more nightmares. Jack eventually moved the family from there, and I got to know him and the lovely gracious Alice quite well through subsequent visits to their various properties. That first consultation with them was the only one in sixteen years that made me cry on the job.

Then one day I had a call from the anguished parents of a teenage son who had suicided. They had rung the ABC Radio for help and, to my later surprise, had been given my number to call. Their painful dilemma was that the son had hung himself from a rafter in the family factory, and they now had to sell the building, but were afraid his tormented soul was still stuck there. A call to the Spiritualist Society had resulted in the advice to light a candle and pray, which had not comforted my clients.

So on a rather grey day I found myself in an industrial area outside a big square warehouse. The parents met me in the carpark. I saw a short middle-aged European couple with thick accents and grief-stricken, worried faces. They were eager to tell me again of their concerns, as they unlocked the building and ushered me into the cold, dark space, now empty apart from a small table with a candle in one corner.

First I cleared the energy of the layer of trauma the place had absorbed, then I tuned in and found the son's spirit was indeed still there. He was overcome with remorse at his impulsive and irreversible action, and the effect on his loving parents. It became obvious to me that a conversation needed to take place between the son and the parents. So with my eyes shut, I acted as go-between or interpreter, while they spoke to each other.

The parents wanted to know why he had done it, he wanted to apologize and they all wanted to express their love. His drastic action had been over an affair of the heart, which now seemed to him so trivial. Tears rolled down the parents' cheeks as the three gradually made some sort of peace. Once this was done the son was able with a little help, to move on.

However, as we were leaving, the Catholic parents voiced their terrible concern to me that due to his suicide, he would surely be destined for hell. Wanting only to allay their fears, I instantly assumed an air of knowledgeable authority and told them this was definitely not so, and that he was now in a wonderful place of peace. I did believe this to be true. This led to quite a discussion about spiritual matters and the afterlife. Fortunately, due to their grief they were wide open and prepared to adapt their religious views to allow them a sense of relief. They reported now feeling ready to sell the building.

For me this was another very moving experience, after which I felt fortunate to have been able to help all three of these people towards a state of peace and resolution.

Hungry Ghosts and the Cappuccino Machine that Refused to Froth

Many of my restaurant consultations yielded earthbound spirits. Did they frequent these places to access food? I was called to a prominent beachside restaurant time and again. One of the reasons seemed to be that they backed onto a public toilet block where drugs were commonly used and there were occasional overdoses. There were also plenty of inebriated, homeless people in the vicinity.

I would be called when the menu printer was misbehaving, or the main oven was turning itself off during a busy mealtime. This was of course quite catastrophic for the smooth running of this large and reputable restaurant. The cleaner at this restaurant admitted he had once actually said, "Good morning," to a spirit, before he realised 'nobody' was there!

Once I had sent off the spirits and cleared any associated entities, all was well again, until the next time. Eventually I appointed an angel to protect the whole restaurant so this would not keep happening. This seemed to work.

I also attended to the restaurant of a client who was having repeated problems with banking. The bank kept losing the cheques to be deposited. Even with a new bank, the same problem happened. I found, and sent off, the spirit of an elderly Chinese man, who had been the cause of the problem.

A few months later, the same client called me about another matter. She told me that there had been no more banking problems after my visit, and in fact that another problem she had not even mentioned to me had also cleared up. Apparently, prior to my visit, the cappuccino machine would not make froth for her, no matter how hard she tried. Only when she asked someone else to do it for her, would the froth eventuate. As soon as I had sent off the spirit, the machine again frothed for her!

Mysterious ways indeed! It reminds me of toilets that stopped dripping, and doorbells that started working after or during my visits. Several times, on ringing the doorbell, the surprised client greeted me with, "That bell hasn't worked for years!"

So just how solid and predictable is what we call 'matter'?

Dark Days, Noises in the Night and 9/11

Just before 2001 dawned, I ran a group in my lounge to prepare us for the new century. We spoke about our hopes and wishes for the coming time, and tried our best to instill energy into them.

I had been leading what felt like two parallel lives for a few years. On one hand enjoying a successful feng shui consultancy, doing spiritual healing, running spiritual development groups, gardening and seeing family and friends. On the other hand it seemed I had got myself entangled with a sinister group with ill motives, and was undergoing psychic attack as well as more concrete attack.

My back neighbour, a friendly woman, was found dying in her house after her mail had piled up in her letterbox for days. Then after she had died, a couple with a howling dog bought the house, and my life started to include dark overtones. My dogs were soon poisoned. As Beau, my huge golden labrador was having seizures on the back step, Finny, my beautiful border-sheltie collie led me round the garden showing me where piles of poisoned meat had been placed. That time they were both saved.

I have since learnt that many if not most people on a spiritual path meet the dark at some stage, and have to navigate their way through it. It haunted my life for many years. If only I could have dealt with it as easily as I dealt with darkness in my clients' lives, but that was not to be.

I heard odd noises in the night, smelt strange smells and files were altered in my study. As I arrived at my clients' houses a car would often pull away. When I returned from work the dogs would be panting with anxiety, jammed up against the side fence waiting for my arrival. I began to feel uncomfortable at night and could not sleep. All in all, I felt vulnerable in my own home and although I was loving my life, wanted to get away or have a man with me for safety and protection. An unashamedly sexist approach!

So my spoken wish in that group for the new century was to have a man in my life. To energise that wish I made a paper cut out of him.

Then came the 11th of September 2001. The world changed suddenly to one of overt fear, division and control, and I felt an urgency to publish that Pleiadian book at last. The time now seemed right and humanity surely needed all the help we could get. I tried to contact the publishers who had originally shown interest, only to find they had gone out of business. Who would publish a book channelled from Pleiadians? Then I recalled that I had a Pleiadian channelled book on my bookshelf, which I had bought after writing mine. I hauled it from the shelf and to my relief found that the publisher, Triad, was in Australia. So this might be easy. The address was in far north Queensland, about 3000 km north of Melbourne. I fished out my old synopsis, added a new cover letter and posted it off without delay.

I soon received a letter back from Peter Erbe, the publisher, requesting the manuscript, which I duly posted.

CHAPTER 9

Peter's Confusing Magnetism

Peter Erbe and a Change of Trajectory

About a week later I was hanging out the washing when the phone rang. I ran inside to answer it.

"Hello Paula. This is Peter Erbe speaking," said a calm male voice. Instantaneously all the air left my lungs, and there was an extraordinary sensation of completion and the whole of life rushing into my solar plexus – the energy of every life form there ever was.

Breathlessly I gasped, "I just ran in from the garden," by way of explanation for the fact that I could hardly speak.

"I know," said Peter quietly. Then, "I received your book and I would like to publish it."

"Oh good," I managed.

"I only take one in a hundred," he said, plainly expecting me to be more pleased.

"Well I'm sure the Pleiadians would be flattered," I replied, gradually recovering my breath and equanimity.

And thus began one of the most confusing times of my life.

Initially it was all about the book. Gradually phone calls took over from emails. Peter and I spoke about the book, but also about our lives. There was something going on which I did not understand. I was magnetized by this man and his peace. Being with him, even on the phone across the vast country, was like being in the presence of God, or one's innermost essence. It fed my soul, even as it confused my mind. His calm words flew like arrows straight into my centre, and his voice was literally music to my ears. Our phone calls often lasted many hours – whether we spoke or not I felt his magnetic presence.

Peter knew things about me that I hadn't told him, and seemed to know what I had been doing, even though I was thousands of kilometres away. After work one day I walked in a forest on the way home. That night he told me he was glad I was doing extra things for my enjoyment. Was he omniscient?

A Pillar of Light, the Cheshire Cat and Disappearing Stars

He often visited me etherically. Once I could feel his essence – impossible to describe – in my house for a week. Then, as I was discussing him with a friend, it left in a trice, as though he had no wish to eavesdrop.

One night I was lying in bed about to drift off, when the bedroom door opened slightly wider and I sensed a figure coming over to me. It was Peter. He merged his chakras with mine – all but the heart. We became an etheric pillar of light. Mentally I asked, "What about the heart?" He put a finger to his lips and left the room. I noticed my sinuses had totally cleared and my whole body felt wonderfully alive.

Sitting in my lounge reading one morning, I felt someone's eyes on me and looked up. There, across the room, I saw a disembodied etheric head, floating in the air, looking at me, or rather through me. Just like the Cheshire Cat in Alice in Wonderland. Again, it seemed to be Peter. I felt embarrassed, rose and left the room.

I spent some time with him up in Queensland, in the beautiful house that he had designed. Every afternoon at four o'clock he would spread a tablecloth on the round table on his large lawn, and make a pot of coffee to cater for the visitors who would show up. They were drawn to his presence, though his words were possibly fewer than his cigarettes. He was a mystery to everyone who knew him well, and made a profound impression on all of us. But he only had friends – no pupils or disciples.

In the evenings he and I reclined on chairs outside, admiring the skyful of bright stars and Peter told me that in the not too distant future, man would see them no more. One day he told me in surprise that he had just seen the events of my life like beads on a string.

I was baffled to discover that he was in his sixties and had chain-smoked from the age of fourteen, yet his voice was beautifully smooth and he had no cough. His explanation was that he 'smoked through the filter of love.'

Of course I assumed this was the man I had asked for in my life. But, to my confusion, he told me I wanted something he could not give me. Looking calmly at me, he simply said, "You are love."

Quantumly Entangled Books, Surrender and Masters of the Far East

His publishing business had only come about due to the spiritual book he had written years before, *God I Am*, which had already sold over 50,000 copies. Grateful readers from across the world often wrote to him, claiming the book had changed their lives for the better. Even though Peter occasionally read me these letters, as I enjoyed hearing them, he remained unmoved by his book's success and effects. He had only written it after his friend, Volker, had asked him to, and he said he had no desire to save or change anyone. He claimed all was perfect just as it was, there were no mistakes, and he would rather have written a symphony.

Curious, I bought a copy of this poetically written book, and on reading it felt inexplicably as though I had written it myself. Maybe we were quantumly entangled after he had merged his chakras with mine.

Peter decided my book was too short and instructed me to channel some more. I had no idea how to do this, when the dictation had come from the Pleiadians. However I made an attempt and many pages came forth.

On reading them to him over the phone, he said thoughtfully, "That sounds like me talking… " I had thought it sounded like him as I received it. This was in 2002. Now this information is in a separate book, called *Riding the Change*, and is highly applicable to dealing with the current times of personal and global change.

Earlier in his life, Peter had had a burning desire to become self-realized. When he was about 40 a technique came to him, which he later found out was the ultimate technique of a certain form of yoga. This practice led to many profound experiences, including levitation, but Peter realised these were merely distractions. He chose to have no more fancy spiritual experiences.

After months of diligent practice, for several hours per day, he was still not realized. So he gave up, defeated, and went to bed at 6.30 p.m. He woke up totally realized and was, he said, 'shown everything'.

That surrender was exactly what had been needed. The pattern of surrender being the doorway to liberation seems quite a common one. As long as one is a seeker, one is bound to the personal. Give that aim up fully and one may be freed from the limitation of personal identity.

Peter had enjoyed the set of books called *The Life and Teachings of the Masters of the Far East*, written in 1924 and 1937 by Baird Spalding, and he suggested I read them. Baird Spalding had been one of a research party to stay in the Far East for a few years from 1894. There they contacted the great masters of the Himalayas and not only learnt from them, but witnessed their amazing lives. These masters, with their astounding superhuman abilities and knowledge, are thought to be assisting and guiding the destiny of humanity. I found these books to be fascinating, and reminiscent of those early books I had read about the Himalayas and Tibet.

Peter told me briefly about his travels to other planets and his friendship with Saint Germaine. He confided one day that if he was a king he wouldn't want anyone to know.

Serendipitous Stories and a One Word Definition of God

During our numerous phone calls, he told me many stories which I have often referred to since, in navigating my own life.

One such story was of his elderly mother. Sitting opposite Peter outside one day, she had held her head, complaining of a headache.

Peter asked her who she was, to which she replied, "I am a little piece of God."

"Can God have a headache?" he asked.

"No, of course not," his mother answered. Her headache was gone in an instant, and she threw away the pills she had been using for other ailments.

Another story was about travelling in a hot deserted part of Kenya in a VW van, when the fan belt broke. Peter had replaced it with first one then the other of his wife's stockings. When the second one broke, they found themselves in the shade of the only tree visible. To their relief there was another VW van parked under that tree and the owners were able to give them a spare fan belt! What are the chances?

A few years later I had an experience of rather similar serendipity. Driving on the freeway at 100 km per hour during rush hour, my Mazda engine simply stopped. The cam belt had gone. I was three lanes away from the verge and just surrendered. Cars were rushing all around me and there was nothing I could do. Yet somehow I watched my car miraculously slide through the various lanes and stop exactly in front of an emergency phone.

Logic would have said that was impossible without an accident. I had not been the architect of that, but the recipient. Similar to the time, decades before, when I found myself changing lanes just before the metal canopy on the utility in front flew off. It would probably have sliced me in half had I stayed in that lane.

Whenever I told Peter how lucky I had been – an angel must have saved me – he said, "It was YOU!"

Peter often told me he didn't want to change me, yet listening to the stories of his life, and absorbing his profound peace and truth, gradually changed my perceptions and motivations. He spoke of God often and it was clear he knew God, while following no religion.

When asked what God actually is, he replied without hesitation, "Life."

"Once you are realized," he said, "You always know what to do." In my confused state I found this an appealing prospect!

He told me the story of how he had once swigged poison by mistake and had been unaffected; and he bemoaned the fact that health-conscious people 'give their power to carrots and beans.'

Crazy Connections, Past Lives and a Quadraphonic Dove Serenade

One night, in silence on the phone together, he transmitted something to me utterly exquisite and indescribable, which went straight into the centre of my soul. It was the first and only time I felt there was actually an anatomy in my soul, which had a definite centre or core. Perhaps this transmission was what they call 'Shaktipat' in Hinduism. This is a spiritual energy transmission from a master to a disciple, in order to facilitate the disciple's spiritual progress. I had no idea I was a disciple and Peter certainly never called himself a master.

Only recently did I learn that in both the Jewish Kabbalah and in the Hindu Vedanta models there are seen to be five layers to the soul, nested one inside the other.

Once I found myself looking out from inside his chest, when he was 3000 kilometers away! He had told me he held me dear in his heart. But surely not literally? I often felt the space inside his feet and had no idea what these strange phenomena meant.

Baffled as to why I felt such a powerful connection with Peter, I looked into whether we had shared past lives together, and was shown many in which we had. We had been children together playing between pillars in Sumeria, wearing white cloth of a texture now unknown. In that lifetime we had later become betrothed, but he had died accidentally by his own sword. It seemed we had almost married time after time, but in each life he had died before that could happen.

I told Peter of many of these lifetimes. In one I had been a slave woman and he had been a skinny illegal boyfriend, who visited me in my dungeon-like room. My master had found him there, knocked him over, then kicked him with his riding boots, rupturing his kidney, which had eventually killed him. As I told him this, Peter felt a sharp pain around the kidney. He claimed he was not psychic as I was. His knowledge was of another sort.

Peter was extreme in his adherence to truth as he knew it, and did not cater to peoples' egos. His truth was so much the opposite of society's that he often rubbed people up the wrong way. He related to the Leonard Cohen song, *Bird on a Wire*, about the difficulty of being free despite the density of the collective. He did not want to hurt or change anyone, yet was determined to be true to himself. These two requirements were not easy bedfellows. Being close to him was quite discombobulating, as I was drawn in at the deepest soul level, yet at the superficial ego level my feathers were ruffled again and again. It was like being pulled apart and having the rug taken from under my life.

At one stage I thought I had had enough confusion and would end this friendship. When I later decided to resume it, doves outside suddenly started a quadraphonic cooing chorus from the north, south, east and west. This relating was meant to continue, I gathered.

I would have whole days of inexpressible sweetness or even ecstasy, unrelated to circumstances. In quiet moments I often smelled Peter's cigarette smoke, from a few thousand kilometres away, or was it with me? Business went from strength to strength. As my perceptions changed it felt rather irrelevant to continue the spiritual development groups I was running, so I gave them up.

I was often told by Peter to just be myself, and that he wanted nothing from me.

My Father and the Red Hearts

My elderly father in South Africa took gravely ill and I booked a flight to go as soon as I could, but also told him on the phone not to wait for me if he needed to depart.

The next evening a little round light played over my camelia bush outside the window. Then close by there were numerous sounds of tiny gumnuts falling onto the Perspex roof outside the back door. Ping! Ping! Ping! It certainly caught my attention and reminded me of the way my father had used a catapult to shoot apricot pips at the birds in my mother's fruit trees. He had obviously passed on and had come to Australia to say goodbye – or hello. There was no other explanation.

(A postscript to this story happened the following year.

I was out all day, eventually arriving home in the dark, and sat down to watch the news. However I was rudely distracted by PING! PING! PING! as tiny gumnuts were shot onto my pergola roof – hundreds of them, and at speed! I listened to the onslaught for a while, bemused, then went outside and stared at this phenomenon. I fetched a torch to light up the tree above to look for possums, but there were none, just the gumnuts shooting down one by one!

I recalled this was how my father had said goodbye to me (or hello, as the case may be) after he passed on, before I left for South Africa. Then I realised the date: the 4th of July, my parents' wedding anniversary! Having always been a stickler for celebrating occasions, he was clearly telling me to wish my mother happy anniversary for him! So I phoned my mother, who was very moved. The gumnuts then stopped.)

When I told Peter my Dad had died and I would be going to South Africa, he sympathetically told me he would be with me all the way. In the plane, already grieving, I was comforted by an invisible hand stroking my head.

Then in Cape Town inexplicable things happened with the tiny, metallic red hearts my daughter had enclosed in the card she had given me to give my mother. These shiny, little red hearts started showing up in all sorts of odd places.

I stayed with my brother, who lived not far from the home for the elderly where my mother was. Having visited my mother, Michael and I were ready to leave, and as I waved to her, I saw one of the red hearts stuck on the car window between us. Another one appeared on the bedside table next to my bed at Michael's house. The following day I walked with my mother to the dining room in her home, and there on the passage floor was another red heart in front of us.

Who had orchestrated all that? If I had asked Peter, he would have said, "It was YOU!" The meaning being: there is only One of us here!

The Cheating Husband, Sun Rainbows and a Shock

Once back home, Peter and I tried to incorporate the original book from the Pleiadians, with the new pages I had channeled, but could not seem to make that work. They were different energies, and about 15 years later became two separate books at last: *The Way Home* and *Riding the Change*.

At some stage during this process, Peter was cheated by an author's husband and was left in dire straits financially. Partly due to this, he lost interest in publishing, and needed to find a quicker way to earn money. I suggested he sell the magnificent furniture that he had built, including the wooden games table with all the different levels, constructed with typical German precision.

"When you fall on hard times, you don't sell the family jewels," was his response. In desperation, tired of surviving on cans of tuna, with little left in his pocket, he asked God what he was to do. He was immediately told 'currency trading', about which he knew very little. I lent him enough money to do a course, and he was soon skilfully trading for wealthy people overseas.

Peter had often spoken of the indescribably beautiful 'garden' or 'paradise' he had spent weeks in, and how he wished he could return there, as he was now living in a dungeon by comparison. He said he had lived seven lives in one life and to me he seemed tired of this life.

"The further up the mountain you travel," he said, "The lonelier it is." I often tried to cheer him up, but my attempts seemed irrelevant.

"No-one knows how I feel inside," he told me, "Not even you."

Like me, others were often angry with him, not understanding his need to adhere to the truth he knew, which did not include what he called 'the fine polish of peoples' egos.'

One evening he stated, as a question I later realized,

"If I left I don't think anyone would miss me."

My problem in this life has been speaking up when I shouldn't and not speaking up when I should, so I let that go. Our communication began to wane, he thanked me for my friendship, told me his love for me was eternal, and hinted he might be going away.

In early 2005 a few weeks later, I was walking my dogs when I saw an odd phenomenon. On either side of the sun, still low in the sky, was a straight vertical band of rainbow. I had never seen anything like it.

Later that day, to my shock and grief, I received news from Volker that Peter had been found dead in his bed. He had led an extraordinary life, had attained spiritual heights and had probably achieved whatever he needed to in this life.

An autopsy showed his death had been of natural causes. Peter had been ready to go, but I missed him terribly. Though I was miserable for myself when he left, I was happy for him, as I knew he was back in his perfect garden with friends of similar understanding, and unhampered by the needs of a physical body and interpersonal niceties.

Rainbows, according to many spiritual traditions, are connected with fully realized beings. I had no doubt that those two rainbows either side of the sun, had something to do with Peter's passing.

Some traditions even espouse that after death our souls enter the sun. This could account for the tunnel of light or the great light that so many describe after near death experiences.

Nature tried to cheer me up in sweet ways. As I sat in the garden feeling bereft, black cockatoos never before seen in my garden, landed a meter away on my birdbath.

I found a nest of baby possums low enough in a creeper to be admired. I went to stay with a friend interstate, and as I drove a flock of pink and grey galahs flew through the center of a rainbow that arced across the road.

Letting Go, Stars and a Red Rose

Peter's friends gathered for a wake, at which they read a piece of my channeling that he had liked:

> Your purpose is outlined in the stars. We do not speak of astrology here. There is an outline for you to fill at some point when you are sufficiently prepared. Nothing else can fill that outline, and you are to be prepared for as long as it takes until you are ready to fill it exactly. This applies to every soul on earth and in the heavens.

We tell you this so you may understand that it is not yourself that creates your destiny. The outline is given to you to fill. It is your birthright as a unique creation. The part you play with your free will is in finding your way to it. It is when you fit it exactly that you feel the sense of oneness with all creation. Striving to feel oneness will not work. Being who you naturally were destined to be will. As you get closer to fitting into the outline assigned to you, everything that does not coincide with its shape must be removed somehow. Either you drop it, or it must be cut off or scraped off. The most painless way is to drop it willingly. The closer you get to fitting your outline, the more urgency there seems to remove what does not fit. When you are still a long way off it hardly seems to matter what shapes you adopt - though some may feel right and others not. Many now, including yourself, are approaching the time of 'fitting their outline.' Thus there is becoming rather a mass sense of urgency in some quarters. This does not help. Any attempts to control and any sense of striving work against all natural processes. So indeed know there is an exciting process at work and allow it to happen. But do not invest time and energy in finding out reams about its workings, in prophesies, in rituals and false timings. It is a naturally occurring flow which only needs your allowance once it reaches this point. All attempts to 'work with' it or second guess its flow merely create weirs. The ride then becomes more bumpy and less graceful, until you realise that you in fact control the flow not at all. All that is required of you is a constant letting go, until you are left with Truth alone. When you realise that what you are letting go of is not essential, it becomes easier. Whatever is essential, is what you keep forever.

Now go on into the light without resisting or trying to control. It is easier that way.

I told Volker about the supernatural experiences I had had relating to Peter, and he admitted he had known there was another side to Peter, but knew none of this side. He suggested I cherish the memories.

I channeled short messages from him to his closest friends, which seemed to bring them comfort.

After his passing Peter and his smoke visited me several times to comfort and check on me. Then about six weeks later, I sensed he was moving further afield, to some other level of being.

Confusion arose in me about whether Peter had actually been a help or a hindrance to me, as he seemed to have turned my life upside down. My friend's partner Tony was a transpersonal therapist and offered me a session to sort out my feelings. I wanted to be released from Peter's magnetism once and for all. But the techniques offered to me in the session did not seem to work. It was as though Peter always came back no matter what I did.

Finally Tony took me into the garden, picked a fresh new red rose and gave it to me saying, "This beautiful rose symbolizes a fresh new relationship you will have with a man."

That evening at home I was reading a book when I heard a 'plop!' The head of that fresh rose, in the vase next to me, fell off in big chunks until there was no rose left! This, I felt, did not bode so well for my future with men!

There was another notable occurrence about ten years after Peter left. I had a framed photograph of him in my bedroom, and decided maybe I should move on and put it away. As soon as I picked it up, there was a loud clap of thunder. It was a calm blue day. I left the photograph where it was.

Peter left me with an irresistible sense of urgency to become realized as he had been; and also with the knowing that being with a man who was not 'awake' would not satisfy me. Very soon I would find I could choose between two 'awake' men. But there would be no-one as profoundly realized, or as challenging to be with, as Peter again.

On writing this book, for the first time in years I smelt his smoke, later realizing it was the anniversary of his passing.

CHAPTER 10

Decoding Masters

Yogananda, Sri Yukteswar and the Jigsaw

In *Autobiography of a Yogi*, Paramhansa Yogananda describes his guru, Sri Yukteswar Giri, in some detail. On reading this description, while writing this book, many puzzle pieces about Peter fell into place for me.

These two profoundly realized men seem to have been similar in many ways – both strict adherents to the truth and consequently with powers, which were not spoken of, and which were employed only when necessary. But while Sri Yukteswar Giri took on the open role of guru, Peter kept his level of attainment under wraps and chose to change no-one. However his being alone seemed to change those brave enough to be close to him, or magnetized enough, as in my case.

Yogananda describes Sri Yukteswar as 'affable and gentle to his guests', but also as harsh towards inveterate egotists, who were 'met with frigid indifference or formidable opposition.' Yogananda suspects that his guru might have been far more sought after had he been less candid in dislodging peoples' egos.

I recall Peter telling me about an American who had read his book and wanted to come and stay with him. After a short phone conversation, Peter had told him coldly to stay at home as he 'wouldn't want to know the truth.'

Peter used to say, "I am *so* simple." Yogananda described his guru as having an aura of 'perfect simplicity'. Apparently Sri Yukteswar seldom spoke of 'superphysical realms' but could secretly perform miracles at times. He had explained: 'A man of realization does not perform any miracle until he receives an inward sanction. God does not wish the secrets of His creation revealed promiscuously. Also every individual in the world has inalienable right to his free will. A saint will not encroach upon that independence.'

Maybe that explained why Peter had immediately withdrawn his essence from my house when I spoke to a friend about him. He was honouring my privacy. And as always he claimed afterwards to know nothing about the whole event! He also said definitively that he was *not* a saint!

Yogananda writes about how it moved him to touch his guru's feet, and about a subtle current that is generated when a disciple is spiritually magnetized by reverent contact with a master. Although I had no background in this life as a disciple to anyone, I had felt a reverence towards Peter's feet which had made no sense to me. I certainly cannot claim to have always acted reverently towards Peter. On the contrary, I had often disagreed with him or been angry with him, yet I had felt that overwhelming magnetic current from our very first conversation.

And as for Peter's ability to appear in my house when his body was 3000 km away, Yogananda has this explanation of how this was possible:

'Let man learn the philosophic truth that there is no material universe; its warp and woof is maya, illusion. Its mirages of reality all break down under analysis… Einstein proved that the energy in any particle of matter is equal to its mass or weight multiplied by the square of the velocity of light… Only a material body whose mass is infinite could equal the velocity of light… The masters who are able to materialize and dematerialize their bodies or any other object, and to move with the velocity of light… have fulfilled the necessary Einsteinian conditions: their mass is infinite. The consciousness of a perfected yogi is effortlessly identified, not with a narrow body, but with the universal structure… A master who through perfect meditation has merged his consciousness with the Creator perceives the cosmical essence as light; to him there is no difference between the light rays composing water and the light rays composing land. Free from matter-consciousness, free from the three dimensions of space, and the fourth dimension of time, a master transfers his body of light with equal ease over the light rays of earth, water, fire or air.'

And I could certainly relate to this: 'Among the trillion mysteries breathing every second the inexplicable air, who may venture to ask that the fathomless nature of a master be instantly grasped!'

The Unwitting Disciple and Very Odd Sleep

'The true value of a human being can be found in the degree to which he has attained liberation from the self.'
– Albert Einstein

I would never have chosen to be anyone's disciple nor would Peter have wanted to be anyone's guru, but some things happen by themselves. He had always said realization was not about 'being good', but purely about a shift of perception. I felt fortunate to have known him, and to have been drawn away from the rather fuzzy path of the New Age, and onto the path of self-realization yielding more definable fruit.

Another odd thing had happened. Shortly after meeting Peter, my ability to sleep seemed to vanish. For years I seemed not to sleep. All night I was aware of the outside noises, and therefore assumed I was awake. Only years later, when I was sharing a room with a friend in Sweden, and mentioned my sleeplessness, was I told I had definitely been asleep. She had heard me snore!

This continuation of awareness during sleep I later found out was a sign of spiritual awakening. At that time, in a few of my dreams I purposely intervened in the action – maybe that was lucid dreaming, which I had never sought.

Some doubts about the merits of feng shui had entered my head, as a result of Peter telling me several times that one can only really help another by 'taking him beyond the need for help.' But my feng shui work continued, and was as fascinating as ever. I felt honoured to be invited into peoples' homes, workplaces and lives, and felt feng shui and I were making a valuable difference to many lives.

The Surprise Cricket Tour, the Frightened Man and a Terrible Tragedy

I had been to the large and well-decorated property of a stockbroker several times before. His wife Penny, a philanthropist, had called me back as they had built a new attic bedroom for Tim, their son. Since Tim had been sleeping in this room, everything seemed to be going wrong for him. He went, according to Penny, 'from one uphill battle to the next with no respite, finally even getting hit on the head with a metal softball bat at school.' His dog, which refused to sleep in the new room, suddenly got a bowel constriction and would not eat. Treatment did not help and to their distress he was fading.

I was greeted by a worried-looking Penny, who led me upstairs to the new room. Here the energy felt awful, and to make matters worse, the bed was under an overbearing sloping ceiling. The configuration of this ceiling was having the effect of chopping Tim's energy field. The softball bat had mirrored this on a concrete level. The energy was cleared and the bed moved to a less constricted position.

Later the same day the dog was taken to the vet, who found the bowel constriction was suddenly gone! The dog had evidently been taking on constriction, on behalf of his constricted owner. An added bonus then happened. In the words of his mother: 'I had rung the school to find out if Tim had any chance of going on the cricket tour to England. They had said no. Suddenly we got the call that they realized that they had lost his original application to go on the tour, and that now they realized it, he was on the tour!! This was a dream come true!' Apparently things truly turned around for Tim and all was well.

Another familiar client, Adriana, called me to ask for an energy clearing as they had had a burglary. She also didn't know why her normally phlegmatic husband, Ben, was suddenly so anxious and could not sleep. They had had the locks changed and there seemed no reason for his level of tension.

On site, as soon as I tuned in, I saw the burglary.

There had been two young men who had broken in more for fun than profit. They had been enjoying looking through Ben's suits and holding them up to the bedroom mirror, when they heard a car in the drive. Understandably, they were terrified of being caught, and scrambled out through a back window just in time. However they left their terror behind, at Ben's side of the bed and all over his suits. Once all this fear energy was cleared, Ben regained his composure and began to sleep well again.

I had been working with the Cipriani family for many years, and had grown fond of them. A close and warm family, they had gradually moved to larger and larger properties, and in the current attractive one had built an office in the garden for their family business. Two children had increased to four, and I had enjoyed following their developments and seeing their design business grow.

The only thing that worried me was their formal lounge. On the wall hung various hunting trophies – the glassy-eyed heads of creatures killed by Dan for sport. I mentioned to him several times that this very much went against the concept of feng shui, which is about living in harmony with the forces of nature.

However the hunting continued, and one winter Dan took his two sons with him on their first hunting trip. If only he had not. They had to cross a river and the younger boy started to get swept away. His brother jumped in to save him, as did their father. Somehow the boys survived, but Dan did not. Jenny, his wife, was left to raise four children and deal with her grief. Dan had been a strapping, amiable, creative man and a good husband, and they had been very happy together.

I saw Jenny again, at the house she later moved into. She was resilient and coping bravely. I felt bad for even thinking it, but I did wonder if nature had exacted some sort of revenge. I'm sure Jenny must have wondered that too.

PART TWO

The Search Inner and Outer

CHAPTER 11

Adventures in Paradise

Scary Nights, a Hot Water Bottle and the Search for an Awake Man

My parallel worlds continued: satisfying consultations by day and a sense of psychic attack and lack of safety at night. There was often the sense of a presence in my bedroom, which felt uncomfortable. My dowsing skills were reliably accurate in my work, but not in the trickiest parts of my personal life. I was too close to the issue and besides I probably had to traverse my dark seas myself, and find my own answers and strengths.

I became alarmed when there seemed to be a presence regularly trying to invade my solar plexus at night. Although I had taught methods of psychic protection in the spiritual development courses I had run, my bag of tricks did not seem strong enough, so I consulted the world wide web for more dire ways of etheric protection. The most lethal I came across was to visualize swirling knives around the body. So I tucked myself into bed on a winter's night with my hot water bottle and set to it with gusto, only to be woken up by a puddle of water in the night. Never let it be said that visualization is not potent – my hot water bottle had been slashed to ribbons!

I vaguely thought of moving house. Peter had informed me that he thought I would be happy near mountains and sea. I was too confused at that stage to know what I wanted! Currently I was in rather flat Melbourne, half an hour from the bay. Now I had the added complication that I only wanted to be with a realized man. I had once offered to lend Peter some books, and he had almost groaned and said he only reads truth, in other words, the work of realized, or enlightened beings. I now felt the same about men. Anyone coming from the usual personal ego position I feared would not interest me. Besides, my primary aim now was to become self-realized.

So onto a dating site I went, and to my surprise found two men at once who both sounded awake. One called himself Silver Scorpio, with a subtitle of 'Fingers pointing to the Moon'; and the other was called 'I am That.' The second sounded too good to be true – living on a remote tropical island. And that name was the name of my currently favourite book, by Nisargadatta Maharaj. Far too good to be true. So I shelved him for the time being, and communicated with Silver Scorpio, who was relatively local.

Silver Scorpio and Non-duality

We communicated via email for weeks before we met. Hans liked the directness of Advaita Vedanta – non-dual Hindu teachings. He had attended satsangs (spiritual gatherings) at Sailor Bob's (Bob Adamson) in a leafy Melbourne suburb close to mine. He had also been to India and attended many meetings with Ramesh Balsekar, until he had what he described as 'a shift of consciousness.' After that he had returned home, and changed much of his life situation. His emails were full of generous, intense and ruthless non-dual wisdom.

'There's nothing bad or evil with thoughts or the mind as such, just don't attach to your thoughts and give them energy.

It is the nature of the mind to start stories and add to them.

You must see from that, that there can never be an answer in the mind.

It's the nature of mind to function in opposites.

Without it we would not experience life.

HOWEVER THEY ARE NOT THE REAL YOU.

THE BASIC FAULT IS THAT YOU BELIEVE YOU ARE THE BODY.

What and where is your body and mind really. Just analyze!

Where is the CENTRE of you? It's a cage of limitations you have built.

It's empty. Dead matter. It has no inherent power of its own.

We are consciousness only.'

And another day:

'All the techniques and meditation in the world will not help one iota.

Sure, meditation certainly helps you feel relaxed, clear and balanced. I still do it occasionally if I'm feeling scattered.

Exercises and meditation without any expectation of experiences or hoping for change is better.

But the expectation is still there in the intention. The ego/mind can be very subtle.

Spiritual ego/materialism is there. All striving actually leads you further away from your goal.

One of the signs of so-called possibility of enlightenment is that you no longer desire spiritual growth; you don't care anymore.

The answer is in letting go, surrendering - undoing all your mind knowledge and belief/concepts.

Yet you can't decide to let go and surrender!

Once you get into the mind you are lost.

It's a paradox.

There really is nothing you can do.

JUST BE WHAT YOU ALREADY ARE.

The ultimate books are those by Wei Wu Wei.

They will destroy your mind! They are the most difficult books I've ever read and I can only take small doses. They are exhausting and not pleasurable, but just confirm the Advaita Philosophy.

You will surrender your spiritual searching after reading them because the mind has nowhere to go ... absolutely no entertainment or bullshit for the mind/ego.'

What he was saying echoed much of what Peter and my channeling had been trying to get through to my addled mind. We eventually met for coffee. I don't think it was just Hans's good looks that kept me riveted to our conversation. There was a deep focus between us, and the rest of the cafe evaporated as we spoke. But there also seemed to be a melancholy about him which I felt would not be good for me.

There is a common misconception that all 'awake' people are the same: sweetness and light, peace and happiness. This is not the case, as people still retain individuality of personality traits and preferences. Hans's difficult childhood had left its mark upon him and he claimed it always would. He spoke of generally being content and was very intelligent, likeable and creative, but there were still patterns active from his challenging childhood which affected him. According to my astrology I have six houses in Leo, and I also have 20 years of experience as a therapist, so I was afraid I might boss him and try to change him. Therefore, although I felt fond of him and we still communicated for many years, on many topics, we only met a few times after that. Hans soon met Diane, who had Buddhist leanings, and they have been partners since.

Some years later Hans was about to go overseas with Diane. He needed to find someone to look after his ageing labrador, Goldie. I asked around and found a kind woman only a few streets from me who loved dogs and was willing, so Hans visited me after dropping Goldie with her. After chatting over tea, I wanted to take his photo. He was a talented photographer and had sent me many beautiful portraits he had taken. When I asked if I could take his photo he muttered something to the effect of 'no-one photographs the photographer.' I said I'd like to take one anyway, outside. To which he responded that he always looks very old in photos.

However I took the photo outside, and to my surprise it was very strange. The image was indeed of an old man, with a face of light and light pouring from the top of his head. It looked more like a spirit than a body. I showed Hans and he quickly said he would let me take one inside, and it would work better. Indeed – the photo taken inside was of the solid, handsome man as Hans usually appeared.

Hans outdoors, with a head of light *Hans indoors, a couple of minutes later*

In future years I was the lucky recipient of many of Hans's travel photos – both fascinating and beautiful. None were as odd as the one I had taken of him!

In the early days of our acquaintance he had sent me a picture of Ramana Maharshi, with his neutral open expression, telling me he wanted to look like that one day. Maybe his intent was already impressing itself upon his soul, which was only visible to the camera.

So, having decided Hans and I would remain in 'friend zone', I contacted I Am That, and that was the start of some high adventure.

My feng shui and healing clients had taught me many valuable lessons. The woman who had bought a farm had followed the wise adage of, 'You cannot discover new oceans unless you have the courage to lose sight of the shore.' I bore this in mind when leaping into my new future.

Almost a year after Peter died my thoughts were still rather unusual. I had made a decision to be 'with an awake man in paradise', whatever that meant. Within a few months I was. This is how it happened.

An Awake Man in Paradise

When I answered his RSVP advertisement, Dietrich had forgotten he was even on RSVP, as no-one else had responded in two years. His aim had originally been to find someone who would help him set up tantra courses on the remote Fijian island where he was living. Early in our correspondence he wrote:

'Perhaps one day you will visit this island, not only because we have connected, but also because of the island's atmosphere and its beautiful people.'

As I read this I wondered if I was manifesting my aim already.

Dietrich enjoyed using his intellect accurately and was precise in his comments about reality.

'I have been interested in meditation, like you, for a long time, and I started to meditate consistently when I was 20. My motive was my yearning for reliable happiness, and I sensed that glimpse of freedom early on that would yield that innate happiness. I learned that we just need to remove

the distractions that keep our attention bound to thought forms. This innate happiness is perhaps what you mean when you say that everyone is good at heart. I don't think a good heart is the result of morality; it is rather a spontaneous outflow of innate happiness or that gentle bliss of infinity. Once this is realised, the good heart can flow again.

From a strictly meditative point of view this could be all that evolution aims for: a sense of fullness that has no definable content, but which is more real than anything else to our awareness. From another point of view, this is the re-kindling of a life that is full with itself. It is the start to a life where every moment is a celebration of itself, and where millions of creative options are at hand. Intuition then will select from these options. In other words, Being will become the foundation for a playground of creativity…'

'As far as techniques are concerned to realise the Being, even here I do not discard techniques as useless (like Krishnamurti did, for example). In fact, I love techniques and find them very effective in discovering the presence of Being. The most beautiful collection of techniques is contained in the appendix of Zen flesh, Zen Bones by Paul Reps. This is a discourse of Siva and Shakti, where he explains those 112 methods of realisation. One is, for example, to observe the turning points of breath – not to miss one for some time.'

'The absence of the awareness of being is produced by identification with something other than infinity… The more you trust life the more you lose doubt and fear of life; you relax. In that relaxation Being reveals itself. Being is life itself. You see that you are life itself.'

'It amazes me how unattractive infinity seems to be for most people. It's like ignoring the bank where we have stored the millions we have been missing in our life story.'

We continued to email and between philosophical discussions, I found out Dietrich, like Peter, had grown up in Germany, had been a professional musician and now had a large string instrument shop. He had built two houses on Koro Island, an idyllic tropical paradise, with a view to setting up a meditation centre there. However at the behest of his Fijian caretaker, Tevita, he was now running a noni juice business, while a manager looked after his Brisbane shop. The noni business was helpful to the Fijians who grew noni trees, as well as to Dietrich's employees who processed the fruit.

Because our email and phone conversations went deep, I trusted the process and the man. He had two horses on the island and stated that when I came to visit we would each ride one through the coconut forest and down to the beach below his houses. It all sounded like a fairy tale and my friends were agog, while my children probably suspected yet another late midlife crisis!

We eventually planned to meet and to travel to Koro Island together from Brisbane. The route to Koro was via a nine hour night ride on a Greek ferry from Suva. When settling on a date he wrote:

'The ferry leaves also around Christmas, no problem. However, no one really knows if the ferry leaves or not until it has left. It may have broken down, the current may be too strong to land, they may change the schedule without warning, but that Wednesday is as safe as any other Wednesday. Wednesday is ok, as there is a plane leaving on Wednesdays too; so in case the ferry doesn't make it, the plane will (most likely - unless it has rained cats and dogs and the grass airstrip is too wet to land.)'

'What an adventure this will be', I thought! I organized my business, found a house sitter for my dogs and garden, and off I flew to Queensland.

A Lucky SD Card and the Maharishi

I stayed for a few days with a friend in Byron Bay, and the first time I actually met Dietrich was when he fetched me from there and drove me to Brisbane. He seemed larger than life physically, energetically and personally, and was warm and inclusive towards everyone he met. We stayed for a few days in an old Queenslander boarding house not far from his tastefully appointed string instrument shop. He seemed very creative and was always on the go.

One day he dropped me at the beautiful, extensive river precinct to explore, while he went back to work. I had ordered a new camera SD card but it had not yet arrived in the post, so I was a bit frustrated at not being able to take photos. After I had wandered around for a half an hour, suddenly Dietrich appeared out of nowhere. How he found me I still have no idea.

He explained, "Your need to take photos was just as valid as my need to work," so he had gone to the post office to check if my SD card had arrived yet, and it had. That little comment of his has influenced me ever since, particularly when I am working and my dog brings me a ball. Is his need to play any less important than my need to work?

Then soon we were off to Fiji. It was very easy to get along with Dietrich – he was always cheerful and friendly. He had in fact written a little book called Reliable Happiness. In his younger days, like the Beatles, he had learnt transcendental meditation from Maharishi Mahesh Yogi, which had stood him in good stead. Now he no longer practiced any form of meditation. It had achieved its objective for him. When I asked him how that felt for him, he described it as 'empty fullness'. He was no longer bothered by thoughts the way most of us are, and experienced an inner spaciousness.

Colourful Washing, Chaos and an Ancient Ferry

The flight to Suva was uneventful, apart from exquisite views of all shades of turquoise and blue above the reefs. On arrival we were picked up by Dietrich's employee there and taken to the rented house where he had an office. One of his enterprises was making biodiesel from the used oil from hotels and resorts. His aim was to reduce the thick pollution from the Suva traffic, and the taxi drivers liked the price. While he worked, I explored on foot, and one day we took a drive into the beautiful lush hills behind Suva. This was the start of my photographs of colourful washing hanging on makeshift lines in the green countryside.

Back in Suva we shopped for supplies – great blocks of cheese and butter, a yoghurt maker and starters, nuts, tins of fish, biscuits and enough other foodstuffs to get us by for months, as there was little in the few island shops. The boxes of food had to be carefully tied up to discourage tampering while down in the hold. Then off to the wharf, which seemed utterly chaotic, with groups of talking people, boxes and ramshackle cars all over, in front of the most ancient ferry I had ever seen. Dietrich had booked a cabin so we would have somewhere to lie down, and finally we managed to find our narrow way there. Most of the passengers had no cabins, but stayed on the deck for the night, as we would do one time when they double-booked our cabin. It was a glorious experience passing the night sliding on the silver water under the indigo starry sky, watched by a fat golden moon.

Letting go of a Horse and a Starlit Forest Drive

This time loud noises alerted us to the fact that we had finally reached Koro, still in the pitch dark. There was much heaving, shouting, clanging and banging of metal and ropes, and the ferry slowly lined itself up against a small, square wooden jetty. There were no buildings to be seen, and the only lights were bright spotlights from the ferry. We stepped out and ages later, when everyone else and the ferry had long departed, were met by Dietrich's tall, strapping caretaker Tevita, and his driver Remy, both very calm from a good deal of kava. I felt like a babe in the woods – everything so dark and foreign – the only lights now those from the utility (small open-backed truck).

Tevita told Dietrich that his horse had died. Dietrich asked what happened and Tevita said he didn't know, and that was that. The issue was never raised again and I marveled at how Dietrich could just let things go and be in the present. Our goods were loaded on the back of the utility, and I chose to sit there too. Then followed an hour long drive I will never forget, on rough road through dark, overhanging rainforest under starlit skies. It was silhouetted magic, the tropical branches like black paper cutouts above me.

By the time we arrived at Dietrich's place, light and colour were beginning to dawn, and I could see the fruit laden trees, the piles of coconuts at the roadside and his two peaked houses perched upon a slope above the coconut forest, with the azure water below. Just below the houses was a large shed, where the noni juice was processed.

The houses were pretty basic inside. One house was the bedroom, bathroom and small study space; the other was more communal with a kitchen and large lounge leading to a net-enclosed deck, and an upstairs sleeping quarter. Both houses over-looked the hypnotic green and blue view below.

Schwarzenegger Coconut, Neighbours and Paw-Paw Flower Cordial

The usually shirtless Tevita, built like Arnold Schwarzenegger, kindly offered me some freshly baked local bread. To my horror it seemed to be crawling with lice. However Dietrich assured me these were only tiny ants.

We soon got into something of a food routine. Each morning Tevita brought me a coconut, which he proceeded to slash open with a machete in his bare hand, once I had drained the milk. Then Dietrich and I would have a delicious breakfast of tropical fruit salad with our homemade yoghurt and fresh coconut flesh. Tevita taught me to cook a local green vegetable which we often included with dinner. He had planted a garden round about the houses, with decorative tropical plants as well as edible ones, and I had brought him some vegetable seeds which pleased him greatly.

Up the hill was a small, attractive round house built by Dietrich's Western friends Caroline and Thom. I soon met them and found them to be both interesting and delightful. Caroline was American and had been instrumental in persuading Al Gore to work towards the end of nuclear testing in the United States. Thom had in his earlier life worked as a feng shui consultant and healer as I did.

They had a phone line, and my only way of contacting the outside world was by a baking hot walk up to their house. For email one had to drive to the other side of the island. At Caroline and Thom's I learnt the cooling joys of pawpaw blossom cordial. Their house overlooked a little picturebook crescent bay, in which nestled the island's only resort. Several Westerners from Hawaii were choosing to move to Koro as a more unspoilt and pristine paradise.

The Happy Bus Driver and the Gashed Foot

The island had thirteen small settlements joined by only one pitted untarred road, which often held young men making kava, children riding their horses home from school, muddy happy pigs or wandering brown dogs. There was no public transport until Dietrich had ordered two vehicles from Japan: one utility and one small bus, which always seemed to be sporting new damage. Young Remy was appointed the bus driver, and would convey his happy passengers all over the island. So Dietrich was much appreciated for this and for the noni business which benefited many villagers, and wherever we went people would shout his name and wave. As he waved back to them I identified with Prince Philip – definitely only the consort.

We had only been there a few days when Dietrich dropped a heavy battery on his foot, gashing it badly. He hurriedly mopped up most of the blood and refused to go to hospital on the other side of the island. Instead he agreed that the bush nurse could help him. So off I went with Remy in the utility in the night through the forest to a distant village, where the helpful male bush nurse gave us bandages and directions. Dietrich was to stay in bed with the foot up for ten days and was to bathe it in salt water twice daily.

So Tevita walked down to the beach daily for the water, and I played nurse, wincing as I dressed the gashed foot. I asked him if it hurt a lot, and he replied casually that there was some sensation there. I noticed he seemed to attach no judgement to this sensation – it was not judged as good or bad. Most of us would have called it pain and judged it as undesirable.

Dietrich was a good patient and suggested I might enjoy a walk with Tevita down to the beach. Walking through the shady coconut forest to the beach was unforgettably delightful, with shards of sunlight slanting through the green fronds, illuminating the numerous fallen coconuts, but I began to feel a little uncomfortable when Tevita started talking about another woman who had enjoyed nude bathing there. He made it clear he wouldn't mind at all and that he was good at massage. On my return I muttered to Dietrich that I was a little concerned that Tevita had designs on me. Not missing a beat, he called Tevita and told him I was not interested. That was the end of that.

Thom came to visit, kindly bringing me much-needed mosquito repellent – a life-saver in this paradise which was spoiled only by these little flying vampires. Thom was another person who seemed to have mastered the ego. He was one of the most gently thoughtful people I had come across, and he and Caroline seemed to be intent upon a life of service, helping the islanders in various ways.

A Striped Swimming Snake, Paradise for Lease and Shining Islanders

Not too far from Dietrich's place was a perfect tropical beach with white sands fringed by swaying coconut palms. Snorkeling there, I was impressed to find the coral reef began only about two meters from the water's edge. I was soon lost in another world among the most colourful fish, tiny multi-coloured Christmas trees of coral and endless underwater darting and swaying visual delights.

Only twice was there a slight problem. Once I scrambled out in a hurry as a large black and white striped snake swam lazily towards me; and the other time I did not exit, as a Fijian man came riding slowly along the beach on horseback and I had nothing on apart from my snorkel gear. The island folk were very modest when it came to swimming. They did so fully clothed and would have been horrified to see me like this. So until he had passed, I stayed down in the water willing it to be opaque, while Dietrich, towelled and on land, acted as decoy.

The Fijian government was selling and leasing a certain amount of land to foreigners, and this beach was one we could possibly have leased for 99 years for a very small sum. We were sorely tempted.

Life is new and rich and wild
Let us love it like a child!

Island life was harmonious between the various villages, most of which were Christian. They had a custom of regularly inviting each other for a feast day. Preparations for this would be a whole village social event – the women cooking together and the men preparing kava and other specialities. They would sing and talk as they worked.

The general happiness and abundance on this island was shiningly obvious, despite the lack of material possessions. The people were rich in community, fresh air, fresh food, freedom and the beauty of nature. The children sparkled with life, and were turned out immaculately for school, and everyone was friendly. There was a police station about the size of an 'Aussie dunny' (old outdoor toilet), under some coconut trees, but I never saw a policeman.

I only discovered one dark side of island life, which might have explained the disappearance of Dietrich's horse. If a man parked his horse on someone else's land, the horse might get his leg slashed in retribution. Horses might recover or they might not. To our dismay we came across one such horse with a deep gash in his foreleg, but still standing.

One block away from Dietrich's land was a very beautiful waterhole said to be owned, but not frequented, by Clint Eastwood. It was an enchanting place overhung by softly weeping trees and with a tall charcoal rocky backdrop. The filtered light dappled the water with deep green mystery and it felt a bit like swimming in a forest cave.

A Sewing Machine, Chickens and a Change of Plans

I decided to civilize the main house by installing curtains and covering the sweaty chairs with pretty fabric. So we caught a ferry to another island where there were shops, bought a small sewing machine, cotton and lots of material and I sewed away. The room duly feminized, Dietrich surveyed my handiwork and with innocent wonder declared it to be a miracle. Meanwhile he bought some very scrawny chickens and built them a house, so in theory we would be able to have eggs.

I admired Dietrich's energy, confidence, creativity and intelligence, but felt none of the magnetism I had felt towards Peter. We got on together very naturally, our adventures between sheets were cosmic, and Dietrich's humorous refrain was 'one day we might find we are compatible.' It was a case of relating in the moment, rather than fixed into a relationship, which can be rather dead. He was full of ideas about how I could occupy my island time if I stayed there with him. We had notions of a book of photographs, and to this end he later bought a good camera. Another idea was using my dowsing skills to find water for bores for the increasing number of Western land owners. To this end he investigated buying a huge drill.

He had given up the idea of calling it Meditation Island and running courses. It was just a bit too remote. There was a tiny grass airstrip and we did fly from Koro once in a six seater, hoping the plane would lift before the finish of the runway, which angled down to the sea. As the plane ran downhill along the grass I photographed a boy on a horse watching from the adjacent forest a few meters away.

After almost 2 months on Koro, Dietrich was obliged to return to Brisbane as his shop manager had unexpectedly resigned. I returned to Melbourne and we flew fortnightly to each other's cities for the weekends. I liked Dietrich, everything logically seemed perfect between us, and my son had sternly told me I would find no-one better, but I did not feel that 'something' that I wanted to feel. I did not yet realize that what I had felt towards Peter was unlikely to be replicated.

CHAPTER 12

The Nature of Reality

A Strange Little Woman all in Pink and Some Bad Omens

There were another couple of wonderful trips to Koro, then, getting fond of him, a few months later I decided to move up to Brisbane to be with Dietrich. I would spend a while there, then if all went well and I liked it, I would sell my house and move up there. So he rented a house for us and put up a fence around the back for my dogs. But already life was telling me this was not to be.

A strange little old woman all dressed in pink appeared twice on my dog walks in the park, and charmingly but purposefully connected with me. Having suggested we sit on a park bench, she gently tried to persuade me not to sell my house or move up with him. I'm sure she was an angel in human form, and for the sake of my future health, I wish I had taken heed.

The night before Dietrich was to fly down so we could drive up together, I had unsettling nightmares that did not bode well. Nevertheless we packed my things and the dogs into the car, and headed north. Twice a tyre punctured, and when we finally arrived at the rental house in Brisbane, my Mazda 626 was too low slung to enter the drive.

Looking back on it now, it was as though life tried its best to tell me not to go up there, but I was determined, and I paid quite a price for that determination. It was downhill from there for me. The ceilings were full of black mold, which Dietrich had not noticed; and visible from the main bedroom was a massive mobile phone tower. He was physically impervious to these environmental challenges, but I was not. I did all I could to get rid of the mold, while he went to work each day. I loved Brisbane, but I felt more and more ill, until one day I decided, with my heart racing at terrifying speed, that if I stayed there any longer I would probably die.

Dietrich was reasonable, as always, and we drove back to Melbourne together. I soon found my thyroid and immune system were in trouble, the relationship faded, and Dietrich soon after married a recently widowed Korean teacher with two small daughters, who had come to his shop to buy a violin.

I might have saved myself a lot of bother if I had known this:

'Whatever is destined not to happen will not happen, try as you may. Whatever is destined to happen will happen, do what you may to prevent it. This is certain. The best course, therefore, is to remain silent.'

– Ramana Maharshi

Mental Maneuvers, a Complaining Neighbour and Profound Perceptions

I was left with wonderful memories and apart from the adventure of it all, had had some profound spiritual experiences in Dietrich's company. Several times while with him, just busy in everyday activities, my thoughts suddenly disappeared into the background and a spacious peace took their place. This sometimes lasted for days, then swapped back when I felt some desire or other. While with him I also came across a shining of my mind that I had not seen before. There is no easy way to describe it, other than an inner shining, which is described in some spiritual literature.

I had also noted that Dietrich seemed to have some unusual power. He had bought a huge photocopy machine for his business in Brisbane. Two men had struggled to get it as far as the front steps of the house, in its large cardboard box. After they had left it below the steps, to my astonishment Dietrich somehow picked it up and carried it up the steps and into the house. How was this possible?

On Koro I had heard him tell the muscular Tevita that his own muscles were like pudding. He always appeared totally relaxed and did not subscribe to any kind of fitness exercises. What I came to understand later is that power is best accessed when blockages to it are removed. This kind of power is not personal and identification with the personal gets in its way.

A year later I asked Dietrich for his ideas about power as related to people – what were his thoughts or feelings about it and how would he define it? I found his answer interesting, typically precise and in some ways reminiscent of Lao Tze.

'On the top level:
I have associated power with relaxation.
The feeling is one of non-entanglement into happenings.
I'd define power as the 'energy aspect of the source of life'.

One level down:
I associate power with concentration
The feeling is one of one-pointedness and success
The definition is 'application and manifestation of divine will'

Another level down (definition):
'application and manifestation of will, inspired by ideals/morality/ethics'

Another level down (definition):
'application and manifestation of will, moved by tradition and unconscious conditioning'

Shadow level - further down:
I associate power with manipulation
The feeling is one of attack and defense
The definition is 'willful self-concern'
So that's my first response...
D'

On another occasion I watched him inexplicably dissolve a neighbour's anger. The neighbour had been annoyed at the noise made by the noni processing, and came to Dietrich's house to complain. Dietrich was welcoming and hospitable as always, and in some mysterious way soon had the complaining neighbour completely jovial and friendly. I do not recall any excuses or arguments, and almost felt disoriented at the speed with which the complainer had been disarmed.

But the most profound experience I had with him was at Caroline and Thom's house on Christmas day. Having enjoyed some cooling paw-paw flower cordial, we sat to meditate in a circle with Caroline and Thom and a couple who had come from Hawaii.

Almost as soon as I shut my eyes, the sense of an I and everything else disappeared and there was only a field unlike anything I had ever come across. There was nothing but an infinitely strong solid substance, compared to which the reality we know was unreal and insubstantial – a mere shadow. The words 'harder than diamond' came to mind as a description of what I was experiencing. I knew this field was all pervasive, and though there seemed to be no movement or form in it, that all forms came from it. It was obvious that this was the only reality, and what we knew as daily reality was as insubstantial as a dream. All the forms we daily sensed, including our bodies, were as flimsy and transparent as a thin veil – completely unreal when compared to this infinitely solid reality.

The meditation ended and I was back in the room with the others. Each person briefly described their experience. When I told of mine, the man from Hawaii exclaimed, "Wow! People meditate all their lives for that!"

Following my usual pattern of not speaking when I should, I remained silent. And for the next ten years I searched for a reference to understand what I had experienced. It was surely omnipresent and omnipotent and probably therefore omniscient. So was it God? Was it qi before it divided into yin and yang? What on earth was it? I mentally berated myself for not asking that Hawaiian man, who had seemed to know.

Then one day, reading *I Am That* by Nisargadetta Maharaj, I came across this, at the start of Chapter 94:

'The world is but the surface of the mind and the mind is infinite. What we call thoughts are just ripples in the mind. When the mind is quiet it reflects reality. When it is motionless through and through, it dissolves and only reality remains. This reality is so concrete, so actual, so much more tangible than mind and matter, that compared to it even diamond is soft like butter. This overwhelming actuality makes the world dreamlike, misty irrelevant.'

So this was what I had stumbled across! Possibly being in the room with some powerfully awake people in a pure environment had set the stage for me to experience this. And since then the world had felt unreal and dreamlike. I found it hard to take mundane life seriously. It seemed as though nothing mattered any more, if it was only a dream.

Since then I have learnt that this is often a stage of awakening, and that one often eventually moves from subscribing to 'nothing matters' to realizing that 'everything matters'.

On re-reading *The Life and Times of the Masters of the Far East* while writing this book, I was struck by repeated reference to 'Universal Mind Substance,' from which all matter was made. This seems to again refer to the substance I had encountered. And Sri Yukteswar Giri refers to 'The Only Real Substance' in his little book, *The Holy Science*.

Over the years of meditating I had had numerous wonderful meditation experiences, as most meditators do. Void, peace, light and so much bliss that once I had apologized to colleagues for grinning so much I was a tad worried

I might be admitted to the psychiatric unit where I worked! This harder-than-diamond experience could not be compared to any other. It was in a league of its own, until a few years later when I had two more almost as profound, which will be mentioned later.

I learnt that these experiences come and go, whereas the truth of being does not, and it is this inner stability of awareness that spiritual seekers aim for. For this reason many spiritual teachers and seekers discount the value of profound spiritual experiences, as Peter had. However they can leave one with the flavours of aspects of truth, and thus can be useful, if not identified with or clung to too much. One cannot make these profound experiences come to order – they seem to be a gift of grace.

> The flow of life will carry you to the transformations you seek if you allow it to. There are many times people resist that flow, and that is what slows evolution (on an individual and global level) and causes suffering. But if you go with the circumstances of your life, realising that they are for the best ultimately, you will evolve smoothly.
>
> If circumstances decree that you must stand up for your rights, you must do so. Having realistically assessed the situation, it is fitting to act in a way that is natural. It is surely natural to fight for one's life if under attack or to seek food if starving. A more unnatural way would be to give up or deny the problem. This would be resisting the flow of life and inviting death and devolution rather than evolution.

Sailor Bob and No Separate Me or You

'When something vibrates, the electrons of the entire universe resonate with it. Everything is connected. The greatest tragedy of human existence is the illusion of separateness.'

– Albert Einstein

Meanwhile I attended several of the gatherings at Sailor Bob's house, which was not far from mine. Bob Adamson spoke of the way Life shapes, patterns and forms as conscious intelligence, and that none of us exist as separate beings, but as consciousness itself.

He invited us to look inside and see if we could find a 'me' anywhere. From the age of about two, we had been conditioned to believe in ourselves as separate people, and this belief, with all the angst involved in supposed separate existence, causes suffering. The separate 'me' is just a conglomerate of conditioned beliefs and thoughts. The real 'me' has never been separate and is universal.

Visitors discussed their perceptions and asked questions. We struggled to comprehend this complete reversal of what we are taught all our lives. Using the mind to go beyond the mind is something of a conundrum – one could almost discern steam rising from some ears!

We hate to disappoint you dear

We hate to disappoint you dear
But there isn't anybody there
What you took to be yourself
Was only a mistaken elf!

There is no solid boundary
'Tween you and what I think is me
We are all the shining stuff
To see the shapes is not enough

This shape is but a hollow shell
A shadow that we know so well
And through it passes life on earth
Tears and laughter, death and birth

Life moulds the shapes to its desires
Shapes the clay and then it fires
We are its puppets but, no fear,
We also are the puppeteer

Bob had woken up to his freedom from the personal self, with all its stories, over thirty years before I first met him. Over time I observed others following suit. The topic of free will often arose.

'Is any decision made which is not a result of every decision ever made since the beginning of time?' I asked myself.

Is there any separate 'me' to make a decision anyway, or does Life, the all pervading field of intelligence, actually make the decisions, and our minds somehow fool themselves into claiming agency? The findings of quantum physics about plasma or a web of spacetime in which none of us are discrete or separate raise similar questions.

'Everything is determined, the beginning as well as the end, by forces over which we have no control... we all dance to a mysterious tune, intoned in the distance by an invisible player.'

– Albert Einstein

I bought a book of Sailor Bob's teachings from him, called *What's Wrong with Right Now if you Don't Think about it?* Once you understand the title, you hardly need to read the book!

Things Are Not As They Used To Be.

Things are not as they used to be
They're so much less solid
And where's the me?

I look around me and all I see
Are forms all made of
The same vast sea.

The Manhunt Continues

After Dietrich, my search for a suitable wide-awake male partner resumed. Surprisingly, I found a string of them on online dating sites. In fact I came across so many it felt like a set-up. Most of these men were merely email correspondents, a couple I met and one I went all the way to San Francisco to meet.

I met Jack online in 2006 soon after Dietrich and I parted ways. He lived in England and described himself as 'not one of the herd' which appealed to me. We were of course too far apart for anything serious to eventuate, but we enjoyed some interesting discussions. I kept his emails, as usual, to use in a future book.

'In 1972 I had an experience of Enlightenment lasting a number of weeks. There was exceptional clarity and I could see many things. I described what I saw to those who were interested. Amongst other things, it was clear to me that we were about to enter an Age of Enlightenment.

Although I felt that I could never lose my insight, one day it occurred to me that this may indeed happen, and I had the desire that, should there be any technique available to 'move' consciousness in that 'direction' then I wanted to know about it. It was clear to me that the Universe had 'understood' my desire. The same day I heard about TM. (Transcendental Meditation)

ALL attempts to train the mind or 'achieve' higher states of consciousness are pointless – any 'effort' runs counter to what is needed. All effort is 'outward' when what is needed is 'inward'. Whilst all descriptions of the state include 'no thoughts', 'inner silence' and so on, these are all the results of that state and NOT ways of achieving it – this is a widespread and fundamental error. The ONLY thing that works is letting go, and I know no way that this is better done than in TM. Of course being in the presence of an enlightened master is also beneficial – though it is worth noting that not all Masters are equal.

It's down to the 'intelligence', but we have so much conditioning that the mind always plays a part and we just don't see that. It's very very subtle. And I write all this as one who hasn't managed it again. But I am very clear about what does NOT work. Life will find a way. That Life / Consciousness / Intelligence simply cannot fail.'

'Communicating with someone who is clearly a genuine 'seeker' and who seems to have a good clear understanding surely can only be a good thing.

Bear in mind, though, that 'experiences' are individual. Discussing these can lead to an increased tendency to think about them, which is not positive. It can strengthen or exercise the identifying with a story.

Funny, I've had Satyananda say things to me that implied he knew something of what had been going on, or had happened, to me. Then when I've asked him about it directly he has said that he did not know. On the other hand Barry Long has looked at me directly and spoken, making it absolutely clear that he did know something. It's a funny world.

The sorts of experiences I had, beginning with '72, were first of all a gradual increasing of clarity until I could 'see' a sort of 'field' (as in magnetic field) linking everything. This field was 'Pure Intelligence' and I referred to it as a field of Intelligence - Maharishi refers to it as a field of 'Creative Intelligence'. Next, I would have specific insights - e.g. I could see that there would be an Age of Enlightenment, there was simply no possibility that this could not happen - followed by what I came to call 'units of knowledge' i.e. the direct and instant communication of some knowledge/idea. This would be done without words - though there might be the odd word which would be 'included'. For instance, after seeing the certainty of the Age of Enlightenment, I immediately received a unit of knowledge confirming this and telling me that I had a 'job to do'. Mind you, I don't know what that is yet !!'

Looking back, what he said about Satyananda echoed my experience with Peter, who had denied knowing anything about the unusual etheric connections we had had. We continued to correspond and share travel photos after Jack found a partner in England.

During these explorations I was still busy with my feng shui work which continued to yield interesting experiences for both me and my clients.

A Visitor to Earth

On one such occasion I was at the home of a client who told me she had not had any mystical or unusual experiences but would like to. As was often the case on these visits, we started conversing about some topics she wanted to explore. She asked if I believed in ETs, and just then something happened that shocked us both.

The house was semi-detached, with a path running down the open side to the front door, and from there to the back garden which was fenced and surrounded by other houses. Beside the front door was a full length window. We both noticed movement at that window and saw a perfectly white figure walking from the direction of the back garden. He stopped to gaze in wonder at a tomato plant in a pot at this window, as though he had never seen such a thing before. As though he had just landed on this planet, in fact.

Maria and I looked at each other, confirmed we had both seen this, then raced to the door, but the figure had gone. We ran out to the road, but again there was no sign of him. Maria said there was no way a person could get into her back garden, unless from the front. There was also no way any human had a perfectly white skin. We came to the conclusion this must have been an ET and Maria was thrilled. He seemed to have shown up exactly in answer to her question.

Both my experiences and the research of others has shown that numerous different races of extraterrestrials visit our planet, with very different forms and appearances. Governments, notably the USA government, have long kept their knowledge about this from the public for various reasons, but it seems it is now leaking out all over the place, to the extent that it is even being spoken of and admitted to by government agencies.

CHAPTER 13

Feng Shui, Children and Pets

Mysticism, Physics and Energy

The vitamins and exercise you take, the air you breathe, the amount of water you drink - these are not the secrets of longevity. The greatest secret of longevity is actually forgiveness. If an individual can manage to hold no grudges against herself, God or others, that individual will be healthy almost no matter what. The mind is the master of the body, not the other way round. The mind is what conditions the energy field which dictates the state of the body. If the mind is continually cleansed of damaging emotions/ thoughts/ wishes, the energy field will be primed to support the body well.

Having been a health professional in my first career, I was naturally drawn to the health aspects of my second. The courses I had studied to prepare for this new career were in various models of feng shui and Western geomancy.

Feng shui is an ancient discipline, thousands of years old, woven of art and science, mysticism, astrology, aesthetics, philosophy, alchemy, shamanism and astronomy. Western geomancy is the study and remediation of earth energies and geopathic stress, which may be caused by such factors as underground water, fault lines and electromagnetic fields. In our feng shui courses we were taught how the lie of the land and building direction, design and contents affect the flow and quality of energy in a building, and how those impact upon the lives of the occupants.

Traditional Chinese Medicine and Chinese martial arts are based upon the understanding that all is energy in flux, including the human body. The insubstantial nature of our visible and supposedly solid reality has since been proved through quantum physics, which now echoes ancient mysticism in many ways.

'Concerning matter, we have been all wrong. What we have called matter is energy, whose vibration has been so lowered as to be perceptible to the senses. Matter is spirit reduced to the point of visibility. There is no matter.'

– Albert Einstein

Our health then depends upon the quality and flow of energy in the body. We learnt that in the built environment there are visible and invisible influences which affect us all. We were taught how to dowse, using a pendulum or wire to find earth energies and how to correct these using copper pipes, coils or other remedies, so they would no longer adversely affect peoples' health. We used scientific meters to measure electromagnetic fields and advised on safe exposure. With the advent and proliferation of radio frequencies and wireless technology this is becoming more complex, often requiring measuring devices unaffordable to most. Astrological models based on a building's date and direction enabled us to gauge the influences a building exerts upon its occupants at different times, and the compatibility between building and occupants.

The subtle fields in which we live mould our lives in ways of which we are usually completely unaware. I found it gratifying to learn a little about this, and to help empower people to steer their lives and health through changing their environments.

Fatal Water and Architectural Adventures

I was often referred clients by naturopaths, including Ladi, who disliked the term 'geomancy' as it reminded him of necromancy! He also felt embarrassed when I identified earthbound spirits at his patients' premises, so he stopped referring people to me. But what can one do?

It was always satisfying to identify the probable cause of someone's ill health and ameliorate it, but unfortunately it was sometimes too late. Sally was a young woman whose husband had cancer of the foot. Pete was only about 25 and this cancer seemed unusual.

I soon discovered he had lived almost all his life in a house with underfloor electric heating. Since childhood his feet had been subjected to an unacceptably high level of magnetic field. I analysed the feng shui in their current home and advised them on all the ways he could avoid future exposure. Sadly, a few years later Sally called me to feng shui the home she had moved into after Pete had died, at barely thirty.

Most cases were happier.

In my early days I used to have stalls at festivals, and I recall one woman seeing my stall from afar and wending her way purposefully towards me.

"Ah," she said, "I really need you. I am a Reiki master, I do all the right things, yet healthwise I am only just keeping my head above water and I don't know why." I had learnt to note the phrases people use and found the reference to water interesting.

Sure enough, at Alison's home in Pearcedale I found an underground water stream under the main bed. Unlike my client, her husband was unaffected. That is typical of geopathic stress – one exposed person may struggle to survive it, while the equally exposed partner may not notice anything amiss. Alison then told me how many of the neighbours were or had been affected by cancer. Some had already died from it. It turned out that there were multiple 'black water' streams running under the area. Polluted 'black water' is notorious for causing cancer in those who live above it.

A few weeks after I had treated the stream with a copper pipe, Alison reported feeling entirely well again. I would have loved to have helped her neighbours, but unfortunately many minds are closed to such possibilities. I popped a brochure into a couple of letter boxes, but heard nothing from them.

Clients' health was sometimes affected by the structure of the building – like the man with the oddly bent passageway, whose painful back was starting to follow suit; the woman with headaches since sleeping under an exposed beam over her head; and the man who felt depressed and confined in his life, while sleeping under a low sloping ceiling in an attic room.

Others were affected by the contents – their symbolism and quantity. A wealthy intellectual man who was trying to write a book just couldn't think, until he had removed a valuable headless sculpture that was in his study. A woman whose house was so cluttered that the energy surely could not flow, found her joints were doing the same, seizing up and blocked.

An artist called me as he could not paint anymore. I found and cleared a leyline carrying guilt running right through his bed. He then told me he had been seeing a psychologist for unexplained feelings of guilt. A couple of weeks after I had cleared this line, he phoned me to report that he felt great, no longer needed the psychologist and was up painting again until late at night.

Couples who could not conceive requested my help, and improving the feng shui of their homes often resulted in pregnancy where all else had failed. Then there were the cases of people affected by what had happened in a building in the past. Without knowing anything about the past, sometimes personality would change, moulded by unseen energy patterns of anger, sorrow or physical symptoms. Once the energy was cleared, the person would go back to their true nature and leave these patterns behind. There was even a woman who suddenly had an urge to take up singing and did so, then was told by neighbours that the previous owner of her house had been a singer.

Of course lifestyle and thinking affect one's health too, but these can be affected by one's environment in ways we are not always aware of.

Lament of the Briefcase

I have served for years now
Following the boss in tow
Politely at his fingertips
Hanging to about his hips

When he enters in the door
He tends to put me on the floor
I have a combination lock
He opens, looking at the clock

I yield to him his documents
And many other odd contents
They seem to me extremely dead
All things he uses in his head

As I sit there I like to dream
Of contents with a different theme
I'd like to throw the papers out
I'll tell you what I dream about

My briefcase soul would like to hold
His bathers, towel and sunbeams gold
I'd take him on a holiday
Somewhere warm and far away

I'd like to see him swim around
With no computer to be found
To sip beneath a green palm tree
A fruity drink and feel quite free

Oh what fun we'd have together
The boss and me in sunny weather
Meanwhile I have to face the facts
I am carrying contracts

But while he has his lunch I can
Dream some more and make a plan
Maybe I could carry some
String instrument that he could strum

We could make music, have a dance
Skip, hop, go backwards then advance
I would enjoy that for a change
if he'd forgo the stock exchange

I do get bored with sitting there
While he computes on office chair
Sometimes while he checks his chart
I fantasize of doing art

I could carry paints and brushes
Mix colours that look rich and luscious
We'd have an easel to paint on
And a tea break with a scone

We might be famous for our art
If we could only make a start
But not to be it seems today
He's picked me up, we're on our way.

Ah well, another day is done
I can't say it has been too fun
But while he plots his business scheme
I can at least sit there and dream

Children Screaming in the Night for Good Reason

The work with childrens' health was particularly satisfying. The invisible influences in our lives range from ordinary to bizarre, and I dealt with quite a range of them.

A family in Beaumaris contacted me as their seven year old son, Robbie, was waking at least four times per night screaming in terror. The parents were understandably distressed and had no idea what to do. They were spiritually aware and Robbie's father often used to talk to angels, but so far this had not helped. In such cases I used to enter the premises and tune in, then could often see a glimpse of the past or feel the tone of what was going on. Otherwise I would go through a list with my dowsing rod to ascertain what was present.

In this case I tuned in to Robbie's bedroom and saw a large male ET in a space suit. I mentally started a conversation with him, asking why he was there. He informed me he was assigned to study that child, to which I replied that he was frightening the child, had no right to be there, and must leave and not return. He refused. So I got out the big guns. When the going got tough I used to work with beings such as angels and ascended masters. Despite my own scepticism and questioning, the proof was always in the pudding. In this case Archangel Michael was called upon and eventually got rid of this uninvited ET researcher.

From that day, Robbie no longer screamed in the night. After a week he told his mother he used to see a big black spider above his head in his room at night. I have learnt that some beings in other dimensions can take on many different forms. It must have been terrifying for a seven year old. He was one of the fortunate ones to have understanding and open-minded parents.

That family had also been having trouble with one set of neighbours, and were pleased to inform me that soon after installing the little mirrors I had suggested, the neighbours had been transferred overseas!

About 10 years later I received an email from Robbie's father with a photo attached. Robbie, as dux of the school, was on the stage receiving his award, and around his head was a large halo! I recalled his mother telling me that in her primary school birds used to alight on Robbie's younger sister. They were an unusually attuned family.

After the experience with Robbie, I came across many other such cases of children being studied by ETs. The child involved was always a particularly sensitive one. I also came across children who resisted going to bed, as they reported seeing ghosts and beings in other dimensions. There were ways to help these children – either by helping the ghosts on, or by strengthening the child's energy field so that it was not quite so open. It was always a comfort to these children, and the parents, to be told that what the children were seeing was real and they weren't crazy, naughty or over imaginative.

One family called me as their baby, Edward, would not sleep. When left in his cot he would scream blue murder. This family lived in a block of flats, and Edward's cot was against the outside wall. To my dismay, on the other side of the wall from his cot, the electricity meters whirred for over a dozen flats. (This was before the days of transmitting meters, so-called 'smart' meters, with their radiofrequency radiation. These are as damaging to health as the earlier meters, if not more so. Whereas the magnetic fields of the older meters attenuate, or reduce, fast with distance, this does not apply to the new meters. They can affect people from much further away. Some people are sensitive to this form of radiation, and these transmitting meters can devastate their sleep, health and life.)

Where Edward's cot was placed, the magnetic field, safe biologically up to about four milligauss, was close to 100 milligauss. Had he slept there every night his chances of not getting cancer or some other serious illness would have been slim. I was horrified to learn his parents had taken him to a sleep clinic which had advised a program of controlled crying. In other words, they were told to leave him there to cry until he gets used to it and sleeps.

By now I had found that if a child really did not want to sleep in his bed there was usually a sound reason. I was all for changing the system. So I contacted the head of a sleep clinic and told him of some of my findings. He was reasonably open and suggested I present him with a formal study of a certain number of cases. Enthusiastic as I was, that type of case then dried up entirely, so my mission to enlighten sleep clinics had to be abandoned.

An Escaping Boy, Disappearing Epilepsy and Troublesome Beds

I was called by a desperate mother who could not work out why her seven year old son kept running away from his bedroom, and even from the house. She described Mikey as behaving like one possessed. He would race from the house, climb over the fence and run away. Yet they were a loving and happy family. It made no sense. I suspected the usual: ETs or spirits disturbing Mikey in his bedroom.

But on parking outside the house I immediately saw, psychically, a black vortex rising from the house. I had never seen such a thing before. Before I even entered the house I was intuitively told what this was all about, and what to do about it. The Earth was attempting to clear its energy, by creating these vortices in various locations to remove dark energy, which had accumulated due to man's abuse or clouded consciousness. I was shown not to close these down, but to etherically create a shield around them, so the dross being removed would not interact with people in the vicinity.

Once I went inside I found, predictably, that the source of this vortex was in Mikey's bedroom. No wonder he had not wanted to be there. Once the vortex had been enclosed, and the energy of the bedroom cleared, his behaviour returned to normal.

Later, on channeling more information about these vortices, I learnt that they only arose on the land of people who respected life and the Earth, and that after the clearing was completed, the spot where the vortex had been would turn into a place of healing. As always with these new strange phenomena, I was a trifle sceptical until I had some sort of corroboration. This came a few months later.

These vortices appeared on several of my regular clients' properties, including in the garden of the McReady family. Months after I had treated this for them, Nick McReady was mowing the lawn one day and was surprised to see sparkling. He described it as tiny lights twinkling on the grass where the vortex had been. It had presumably changed to a place of healing.

At the time I had been organizing groups of an Earth-healing nature, which were running in several countries. After seeing these vortices and realizing the Earth knew how to heal herself, I stopped all those groups, lest we interfere with a natural process. I had been informed via my channeling that these vortices were now on many continents, gradually spreading across the world and clearing much accumulated negative energy.

I was regularly surprised by the results of the interplay of place and person. A new client, Norma, was showing me through her large, modern home in Bentleigh, when she happened to mention that her eight year old son Sammy had recently developed epilepsy. His bed, I discovered, was in a low energy position, and worse, the head of his bed was directly in front of a low passage light on the other side of the wall. I strongly suggested she move his bed.

A few months later, Norma wrote to me to tell me that since Sammy's bed had been moved he had had no further epileptic attacks. It seemed the electric current behind his head had been enough to muddle his brain's delicate electrical impulses.

The bed positions of children have a large bearing on how they develop. The most supportive bed position is diagonally opposite the door, but not against a window. Time and again, I found children whose beds were moved to a supportive position had growth spurts, became more confident or improved at school. Some bed positions can be tiring (head on the same wall as the door, or under a window); some anxiety-provoking (directly opposite the door); while others are relaxing and nurturing.

An interesting case was a pair of identical twins – the one in the good bed position was thriving while the other was struggling. After changing the bed positions to support both of them, the previously disadvantaged child soon caught up.

Feng shui does not only benefit people. All creatures are affected by the quality, quantity and flow of energy in their environment. And all creatures and objects in an environment in turn affect that energy.

Heroic Dogs, a Miffed Cat and Lethargic Racehorses

There is a Chinese belief that if your goldfish dies, it might be saving you from illness or misfortune. According to my experience, this probably applies to many of our pets.

Early on in my feng shui career I received referrals from a well-informed vet, who realized that pets too, can be greatly affected by their homes. I was surprised to find that some dogs tend to take on the damaging negative energy of a place in order to protect their owners.

A prominent dog trainer could not understand why his German Shepherds, one after the other, were succumbing to cancer. I suspected that perhaps the owner had placed the dogs' beds next to the fridge or freezer, where there is a high magnetic field.

However, on my visit I soon saw this was not the case. On dowsing, I found that there was an underground water stream running below the house and right under my client's bed. This particular kind of stream can cause health issues such as cancer, for those sleeping above. Both the type of pollution of the water, and the electric current created by the flow radiate up to affect the person above.

The client's health, however, was fine, because the dogs were sleeping upstream of where his bed was and taking the sting out of the stream for him. No-one knows the intricacies of how this works, except perhaps the dogs, but it does. By hammering a certain length of copper pipe into an exact spot, I was able to remove the effect of the stream, thus freeing the dogs from their heroic duties.

There was a similar case of doggy heroism, with an entirely different cause at a house in Ringwood. The dog was not even mentioned until I was busy with the consultation, and the client and I were chatting. Amina happened to mention that her little white dog, Fluffy, had not long to live. According to the vet her kidneys were failing and she might only have a couple of weeks left. By then I was already starting to feel a bit sick, due to the awful dense energy of the house. In this case it was due to past emotion and events, held in the memory of the energy field. The feeling was suffocating and nauseating.

So I cleared the energy, bringing back a lightness and freshness. Instantly Fluffy was at my feet, eyes filled with gratitude and tail wagging. I realized she had been taking the bad energy onto herself for the sake of her family.

Sure enough, Amina phoned me back a fortnight later and told me that on her visit to the vet he had been astounded that there was no more sign of kidney trouble.

Fluffy went on to live healthily for several more years, and it became quite a common event that once I had cleared the energy of a place, the pets would come and thank me. Even pets normally reserved with strangers, would lavish affection upon me, to the surprise of their owners. Many of them also seemed to see the energy around my dowsing rod and would stare at it with great interest.

Another client told me her little dog, Coco, was behaving strangely, was loath to leave the couch in the lounge and would not even get down to eat. I found a vortex in the lounge, which was exuding harmful energies. As soon as I had removed the effect of this vortex, Coco stepped down and became his old self again, coming to thank me when I left!

A sad story happened recently to an elderly acquaintance of mine, who was not open to my feng shui suggestions. The design of Andrea's attractive beachside home was very unsupportive of good health, and she had recently added wifi, again a challenge to health. Her beloved dog, Millie, got cancer and died after a few months. I suspected that Millie had taken the cancer to save her owner, and that Andrea, who had had cancer in her childhood, might now not last long herself. Sure enough, soon after Millie passed, Andrea was diagnosed with cancer, and succumbed to it the same year.

Even my dogs did their bit for me. I thought I was coming down with a cold at one stage. Then my slight symptoms disappeared and Beau, my labrador started coughing. His cold lasted about three days, then Finny, the collie cross, took over and coughed for about a week. I never did get that cold!

So when your dogs are unwell they might be saving you from illness. I gathered no evidence that cats are as altruistic, but of course that does not mean there are no selfless cats around, despite their rather self-indulgent reputation!

An amusing incident occurred with a client's cat. Things were recently not going well for Janet, a nurse educator who had used my services for years. She lived in a lovely old apartment, surrounded by gardens lovingly tended by one of the residents. The neighbour on the other side of the wall behind Janet's bed had recently been replaced by a new one. It was more or less since then that things had taken a downturn for Janet. At work she was being scape-goated unjustly and was in danger of losing her job.

On tuning in, I found that the energy passing through that wall from the new neighbour was heavy and conflicted. I told Janet that I would clear the energy on her side, then we would install small mirrors to deflect it from re-entering her bedroom. Her large cat, Pansy, was stretched out luxuriously on the bed, savouring the comfort of a daytime nap on a soft blanket. I warned Janet that when I had cleared the energy Pansy might be put out, as cat's, unlike dogs, often lap up what we regard as negative energy. On cue, exactly as I cleared the energy, Pansy rose up, shot me a very dirty, accusing look and stalked out of the room, flicking her tail in disgust!

All species are directly affected by the energy flow and quality in their environments. The racehorses at a large horse stud were lethargic and unsuccessful for a completely different reason. Their stables were placed in two rows facing each other with a thoroughfare between. The energy was racing straight through that thoroughfare, instead of entering their stalls and supporting them. In this case the cure was a large metal wind chime in the centre and a hedge at one end to stop the through flow. Once this was in place, the energy meandered into their stalls and it wasn't long before they picked up and started to win races again.

Out of 365 days of the year I happened to have arrived at this horse stud on the annual day the foals were separated from their mothers, and I was privy to the loud cries of horsey grief all round. Strong emotion such as this often makes its mark upon the energy field and may foster future unfortunate events. So we discussed the possible use of lavender oil to calm the horses, and various ways to help clear the energy after this annual traumatic separation.

At another horse stud, staff were suddenly falling off horses, due to 'falling energy' in a stable from a horse, which had been traumatised from a bad fall. Once both the entity and the energy created by the trauma were cleared, there was no more falling.

CHAPTER 14

Ecstasy and Sudden Change

San Francisco, Esalen, Bears and Toothpaste

I don't give up easily. So it was back to Spirit Singles, a dating site, late in 2006, where I discovered a man who called himself, 'Tall, Handsome and Awake'.

'What's not to like?' I thought, 'Except that he is in the USA and I am here in the Land Downunder.'

Nonetheless we engaged in email conversations on my favourite topic, as Jim Dreaver turned out to be a teacher of awakening. He had grown up in New Zealand, moved to California, became a chiropractor, and having been inspired by teachings of J. Krishnamurti, had sought inner freedom. This he had eventually attained in 1995 with the help of non-dual teacher, Jean Klein.

Now his main aim was to help others find their freedom from identification with the personal self, with all its accompanying angst. He was very clear and simple in his communication.

In one of our many emails I told him about my strange and confusing journey with Peter. His response was:

'So, writing it down, re-telling yourself the whole story, is a very good way of getting free of it... then it will just be a beautiful story about this man you had the great fortune to know and love, but 'you' won't get lost in it... after all, the 'you' who still has a tendency to get lost is the final illusion to be gotten free of...'

'The journey of awakening is the most important we will ever make. It brings freedom from self-doubt, anxiety, worry, resentment, blame, the fear of being judged, and others being able to push your buttons. It results in your not taking things personally anymore, because you're no longer identified with this 'I,' this 'me' and its many 'stories' of expectation and disappointment, of gain and loss, of pleasure and suffering.

Freedom unfolds as you see that this 'I,' or 'self/person' you've believed yourself to be all these years doesn't actually exist — when you look for it, it can't be found — yet you, as the awareness behind it all, are very much here.'

'The teaching itself is simple. It is to grasp that while we are a story-telling people, the stories we tell come and go, they change, but we, in our essence, are always here. We, as the pure awareness that sees and knows are still here, still looking through our eyes, sensing with our body, feeling with our heart and gut.

Realizing we are that which is always present, and not the thought or story, which is ever-changing, is to be awake and free.'

'There is a simple yet potent practice for transforming personal suffering

into clarity, harmony, and new creative energy. Whenever upset arises, take a few moments to become fully present. Feel what's happening inside you. Look for the 'story' you are telling yourself that keeps the emotion alive. Then breathe. Let your energy expand. Be very aware. Notice how you can look at the story, so you can't be it. You are what is looking—clear, vibrant, present-time consciousness. Get this, and a shift happens. The story loses its power over you, and you are free.

Do this often enough, and you'll question the very 'me' you take yourself to be. You'll see that it is just a 'story' too, the story-teller, and that your true nature is the lucid, ever-present consciousness behind everything. To know this, to find your identity not in stories but in the moment-by-moment flow of being, is true freedom. It's what it means to be awake, enlightened, or self-realized. Then life is always rich in love, meaning, and purpose.'

For many years Jim has run an annual awakening course at Esalen Institute, on Big Sur, in California. Esalen was founded in 1962 – one of the early formative centres of the human potential movement. After communicating with Jim for a few weeks, I decided I would like to go to California to meet him and participate in his course.

I flew to San Francisco, where I spent a couple of nights in a youth hostel, checking out Fisherman's Wharf, Chinatown and the Golden Gate bridge; trying clam chowder and riding trolleybuses up steep roads. Then Jim fetched me and off we drove down the ruggedly scenic Big Sur to Esalen Institute.

Esalen is a beautiful place, with colourful edible and ornamental gardens, and huge cedar trees perched on a cliff above the crashing ocean. I shared a cottage with another female participant. Our classes were held in a lovely room with a roaring fire, or outside on the lawn when we warmed up with qigong. Meals were a treat in the big communal dining room where we helped ourselves to delicious organic vegetarian food. Here I met and fell for quinoa.

The whole event was most enjoyable, including a lush forest walk, creative fun in the art room, a group nude evening spa on a cliff overlooking the ocean and a surprise outdoor concert from Joan Baez herself! During the course sessions, some participants seemed to have breakthroughs, and were able to release grief or other problems and move on into greater freedom.

After the course, Jim and I drove to Yosemite National Park as planned. We arrived at night and had to find our tent in the dark between black trees. Everywhere were warnings about bears: 'Don't leave your toothpaste or other toiletries in your tent as bears might smell it!' This was a great novelty for someone from the southern hemisphere! We dutifully put all our perfumed items and food into lockers away from the tent.

By day we explored this awe-inspiring park. We saw apparently tiny intrepid climbers attacking El Capitan – the huge vertical rock face – and walked between ancient, towering, giant sequoia trees. The views were stunning, but I also noticed something else.

My relating with awake men had shown me that of course they were all different, as are we all. Jim brought another dimension to this. He seemed to have around him a sort of palpable aura of harmony – almost like cotton wool. I don't know whether everyone would have felt it, but I certainly did.

This was another wonderful trip with a wonderful new friend. Jim has written many books, has individual sessions with people, speaks to groups and sends out a newsletter. He now lives in Los Angeles with his partner.

> All dependence on the future and the past must be relinquished if you wish to be truly free.

The Ecstasy of Life

"Our ancestry stretches back through the life forms and into the stars, back into the beginnings of the primeval fireball. This universe is a single multiform energetic unfolding of matter, mind, intelligence and life.'

– Brian Swimme, cosmologist

While I enjoyed my work and tried to ignore noises in the night and other strange trials at home, my spiritual life continued to unfold. One evening in 2007, I was admiring the stars when suddenly everything changed.

There was no me or world, just Life itself fountaining out and out in an ecstasy of infinite and eternal becoming. And I was It. At the same time, although there was no consciousness of a body, I could feel the starlight coursing through my veins.

I do not recall how long this experience lasted – probably only minutes – but the effect upon my consciousness was immeasurable. It remains the most ecstatic experience I have ever had. The ecstasy was inexpressible yet gave birth to many poems. For days afterwards I sat with words pouring from my pen. I felt I had touched the essence of life itself, and with that came some glimmer of understanding. This fountaining of life was behind and throughout everything and was one. There could not possibly be any division in it. Nor could there be time. It was only ever eternally present, and eternally fresh and new.

This Present Moment

This present moment
Holds the sweet promise of all within its horizons.
All that ever was or will be is held within its thrall:
Every song ever sung,
Every leaf ever moved,
Every breath ever sighed,
Whispering forever into the rainbow winds of eternity,
Ushering in possibilities undreamt.

How can this sweet ecstasy not explode into itself once more,
As stars pulse their shining rhythms
Through these mortal veins?

The potential of every possibility in creation is felt
In the form of a spinning dance,
Whirling as the galaxies forming
Uncountable combinations of colours at play -
Mischievous hints,
Ravishing promises
Peeps behind pillars
Of tomorrows unformed as yet.

We dance on tiptoes between stars revolving,
Our balancing none of our doing;
Light shining with blinding effusion regardless
Of whether I've ordered the dogfood.

The present moment holds eternal life captive
In motionless motion,
In crashing silence,
Expanding, bursting, radiantly one.

Thank you for this Infinite Eternal Play

Thank you for this infinite eternal play
Surging through these veins to the stars,
Dancing beyond and back,
Flinging stardust around infinity.

I am the cause and the result of all –
This bursting heart cannot hold
The expanding thrust that would encompass galaxies,
Melt the sun and devour the dark.

This endless moment holds all others in its palm
Lightly as a feather holds the bird.
This bubbling life ... this fountain of power
With shining energy plays only with itself.

Engulfing itself in endless motion
An eternal writhing dance of gods
Overflowing, speechless, formless,
Ever-new electric ecstasy.

This present moment leaves no room
For anything but song
Beginningless and endless,
Drowning all in its mighty merciless flow

Where are the boundaries?
Colours of silence, choirs of light
What is in and what is out?
One endless dancing field of bliss
Bursting eternally into itself.

There is nothing else.

There is Nothing Here

There is nothing here
In this all-encompassing explosion.
Perpetual dynamite
Showering upon itself
The grandness of possibility –
A myriad of illusory light-plays
Forming Shakespeare's stage,
Laughing as they explode again
Into ever-new forms,
Evolving from nothing to nothing
Rolling in amazement as they contort
Into shapes undreamt of.

Go back a step
And the Watcher is but peace,
Issuing from a boundless heart:
An overwhelming silent love
Greater than all that issues forth
As its creation –
The silent Dancer of the dance
And yet the Dance itself.

Who is to say what is Dance
And what is Dancer?
There is no-one here to observe
And decree from afar –
No-one even near,
No-one at all.

Just the Dance,
Giggling through itself –
Each glimpse of Life a delight,
A glory unto itself
Each story a realm of satisfaction,
A beginning and its own completion.

Nothing undone.
Nothing left out.
Nothing sought.
Nothing mistaken.

I had seen that Life was the primary force that flowed through everything, joyously, with no distinctions and no ceasing. And that we were It.

Yet the mundane still seemed to surround me, with its question marks.

> There's the idea that I am extending creation by expressing myself fully, adding to it all in terms of quality and quantity, and that this is my duty as a person with a life on earth.
>
> You will be doing this just by being. There is no need to add anything artificial on top of this. Being is sufficient.
>
> So we are talking about being in the present moment without regard for a future or a past. Allowing the creation of oneself to emerge from the inside and in the present. Allowing life to emerge from within, where it is, rather than imposing ideas about how it should be, from the mind, which is stultifying. A very alive feeling comes with that. Every moment is thus a new surprise, as opposed to something pre-planned and stale. Like a flower constantly blossoming.
>
> And I am the one that watches this blossoming as it occurs. So no-one orchestrates it. It occurs and I watch it. Effortless. Life lives itself through me, and I can watch the play. The body-mind performs and I observe.

Life Takes the Reins, an Ending and a Beginning

No matter how transcendent the experiences, it was easy to help my clients, but not always as easy to help myself, as is often the way. The feng shui of any building is subject to changes with cycles of time, and I knew that after early

2004 my house would not serve me as well as it had. I thought of moving, but was not clear on where to go, and assumed I would not be able to rent while deciding, due to my two beautiful dogs.

So I procrastinated until finally Life stepped in, as It does. My trials at home culminated in my dogs both being poisoned, one two weeks after the other. This time it was successful and I lost them both. Finny and Beau had been wonderful dogs and were both perfectly healthy at thirteen. Devastated, I ran away for a few weeks to friends interstate.

On my return I realized it was time to move, and that, as Peter had said, I wanted to be near the sea. Then again Life seemed to take over. Is It ever not in charge? Searching online, I found a house I liked the look of, and decided to drive down there via some other beachside suburbs, viewing a few more houses on the way.

At the first beachside suburb I turned into, with no warning, I had an urgent toilet call. It was as though I was being symbolically purged of my past to make way for a new beginning. So I went straight to the house I had seen online. The owners just happened to be outside chatting to the neighbour, and offered to show me around. I liked it, showed it to my children the following weekend, then bought it.

Good Grief! How Did That Happen?

Soon after moving to my new semi-rural beachside home, I realised I was sixty and I remembered something which gave me goosebumps.

In primary school we were asked to write a composition called, 'When I am sixty…' I had written about my beloved grandmother and how I would like to be like her when I am sixty. She had lived about an hour from our family, in the country; and my brother, cousins and I had all enjoyed staying for holidays with her. At about ten years old, I wrote that one day I would like to provide similar country holidays for my own grandchildren.

Now here I was at 60 and I had just moved an hour from the family, into the country, with a view to having grandchildren to stay. I had done that without consciously realizing I had planned it all 50 years before! That plan had been sitting in my subconscious for most of my life. At that stage I already had one grandtoddler. Now I have four grandchildren and the plan has come to fruition.

> Let your life fall into you like raindrops into a parched land. Soak it up willingly and gratefully, knowing you are getting exactly what you have asked for.

In 2012 I had a rather similar sense of surprise. Even though I had lived longer in Australia than in South Africa by that time, I still struggled with an Australian identity. Initially we had planned to emigrate to Canada, but had changed our minds due to the cold climate there. Though there was much I liked about Australia, at some deep level it still didn't resonate with me. I felt more drawn to all things South African or even Canadian still. So I thought perhaps I could change that by going to Uluru – the huge rock at the centre of Australia, previously known as Ayers Rock.

This enormous edifice which rises abruptly from an endlessly flat horizon, is seen as the spiritual centre of Australia. Maybe here I could catch the soul of this country. With this in mind, I joined a small group travelling to Central Australia. We flew to Alice Springs, then hired a car. The amazement struck when I saw the registration plate of the car: CA28OZ.

CA is the beginning of all car registration plates in Cape Town, where I came from. And I had been 28 when I emigrated to OZ – Australia! If that wasn't some sort of symbolic joining of my two national identities around me, then I don't know! What sort of cosmic intelligence orchestrates something like that?

I fell in love with the beauty of Central Australia. This desert land is also called the Red Centre due to the striking soil colour. Its vast landscapes are varied and magnificent. There are the endless desert plains dotted with scrub; and iconic rock formations, the most famous of which are Uluru and, 40 kilometers away, Kata Tjuta, formerly known as The Olgas. Kata Tjuta, meaning 'Many Heads' is a breathtakingly strange collection of 36 smooth ochre-coloured dome-shaped rocks, sacred to the local Aboriginal Anangu people who have inhabited the area for over 22,000 years. The tallest dome, Mount Olga, is 200 meters taller than Uluru. We meandered through the Kata Tjuta National Park, marvelling at unexpected pockets of greenery, including ancient moss-festooned tree ferns, among these weird shaped rocks.

As Uluru is sacred to the local people, tourists are now banned from climbing on it. Instead we walked the 9.4 km circumference of it, dwarfed beneath its massive bulk. It is 348 meters high and, like Kata Tjuta, 500 million years old – twice as old as the dinosaurs. Originally the whole rock was under water, until the seas receded 400 million years ago, leaving it standing there in all its glory. Standing under it at sunset was an unforgettable experience. The whole steep rock face turned yellow, then orange, then vermillion. It seemed to glow from inside.

Due to our tour leader's connections, we were fortunate to spend time with Uncle Bob Randall, a well-known Aboriginal elder, author, songwriter, musician and long-time activist in Mutitjulu, the Aboriginal community at Uluru, which is kept private from tourists. The word 'Uncle' is used as a symbol of respect.

We spent the day with Uncle Bob at his home in Mutitjulu. I was interested to see large pictures representing many different religions on the walls of his home – Jesus, Buddha and others I do not now recall. We were shown *Kanyini*, a highly acclaimed movie which he had narrated and co-produced, and were deeply moved to learn more of the difficult Aboriginal experiences in this, their own land. Accompanied by his guitar, he sang his 1970 song, *My Brown Skin Baby They Take 'im Away*, which had become an anthem for the Stolen Generations – those people forcibly removed as children from their families, due to their skin color.

Uncle Bob had been taken from his family at about seven, due to having been 'half-caste' – with a white landowner father and an indigenous servant mother. Between the 1910's and the 1970's, the government took hundreds of such children from their families and lands to raise them in institutions as whites, believing this was best for them. Here they were forced to abandon all their language and traditions, and to speak English – a move causing ongoing multi-generational trauma, for which a formal government apology was made in 2008.

Uncle Bob lived in such institutions until the age of twenty, then spent the rest of his life doing all he could to restore the Aboriginal culture to its rightful place, and to gain equal rights for Aboriginal people. He became an Aboriginal cultural educator and established many centres around Australia. He authored four books, including *Songman*, his life story. Despite such traumatic beginnings, his life was one of huge achievements, dedication and creativity.

We met again with Uncle Bob and his brown dog to view 'The Rock' at sunrise, another glorious sight of exploding light, gentler than sunset.

Our timing was lucky, as only three years later Uncle Bob passed away, at the age of about 81.

We explored Alice Springs, a town rich in colourful Aboriginal artworks. None of us could resist buying dot paintings from street sellers. We visited large art workshops which housed Aboriginal women artists painting away from large pots of colour. There has been much financial abuse of these artists, who have been paid a pittance for paintings later sold for thousands of dollars, since international recognition of Aboriginal art took hold. Hopefully now there is more regulation of this trade, so the artists receive their due.

Then we drove to the McDonnell Ranges, where we explored many dramatically beautiful gorges. I have photographs of white trunked eucalypts dangling grey-green leaves in front of glimpses of shining blue water, walled in by towering red rocks. One of the outstanding aspects of Central Australia is the rich colour one is bathed in everywhere. It is a land which shouts quietly and powerfully.

All in all it was a wonderful trip, and a view into a very different and vast Australia. I'm not sure that it put Australia into my centre, but it must have helped.

Majesty and Grandeur

When I was about 40
And I'd been in Aus
For twelve years
I went to a psychologist
"I miss Africa terribly", I told him
"What is it you miss?" asked he
"The majesty of the mountains
The grandeur of the animals"
(They're a bit quirky in Aus)
Said I

"Hmm," said he, stroking his chin
"Majesty and grandeur?
But you already have those
Within you."
"Ah! Of course!" said I.
"I had forgotten."
And I never saw him again.

CHAPTER 15

Miracles and the Sanity of Dogs

Who Dunnit? Another Mystery

Alex, the elderly man who had sold me my house, had described how he used to fish in the dam up the road for carp, which he would dig into his vegetable garden. I aimed to grow vegetables too, and he asked me what I would like him to plant for my use.

After I moved in, the vegetable patch appeared to consist only of bare soil. I naturally assumed in the busyness of moving Alex had forgotten his promise to plant vegetables for me. At the time we were at the tail end of a twelve year drought and any unwatered garden was bone dry. Yet each morning for about ten days I found a strip of that bare earth had been watered! Alex could not have sneaked back nightly to water, as he was now living over a thousand kilometers away in Queensland.

After the tenth day, tiny green seedlings began to emerge – a row of carrots and one of spinach. So Alex had fulfilled his promise! But who had been watering? It was certainly not neighbours, who had no access. I was again thrown into confusion. Was it the angels I sometimes worked with? Was it earthbound souls I had helped? Was it Pan himself or his nature spirits? My ET friends? Or even Peter from beyond? At times like this my dowsing and channeling were opaque. I had to manage my own mysteries without their aid. At the time of writing, I still have no idea how that soil was watered.

Oh for Solid Normality!

Even though these experiences were gifts, sometimes I found them quite distressing as I could not explain them. Whenever I had the opportunity to ask someone more spiritually advanced about them, I did. Tibetan lamas, shamen and Aboriginal elders were all accosted about my confusion, but the only answers I received amounted to the fact that 'it was good.' Min Mla, an Aboriginal elder did suggest I might be a 'wirrloo', which I understood to be a teacher or healer.

I made an appointment with the psychic spiritual counsellor of a client to discuss my questions. Her answer to all my strange happenings was: "You are very powerful." I still didn't get it. I went to a swami to ask about my strange life and about Peter. My strange and mystical powers had come from spiritual development in past lives, he said. He told me Peter had been and still was my guru, and I should put up an altar to him with a photo and flowers. I knew Peter would have hated that idea, as did I.

When I was woken in the night by knocking, a bell ringing, or a strange smell, I had no idea if it was from friend or foe. Were the ETs I had banished from childrens' bedrooms coming to punish me? Were the drug dealers from over the road trespassing to make mischief? Was it a test of my fearlessness, or to make me stronger? What was I to make of it?

At one stage, tired of dealing so much with unseen realms in my channeling, work and nights at home, I shut the door to them all. I no longer wanted to be called out to dance in the moonlight by nature spirits, channel for beings that had something to say, or even believe in other realms – be they guides, angels or Ascended Masters. I just wanted a grounded, ordinary life that I could make sense of. Besides, my deeper spiritual experiences had shown me something beyond all the New Age talk of self- development, crystals and spiritual guides. I felt I had seen beyond the phenomenal manifest world, visible as well as invisible, and did not want to be bound by its edicts. I only realised later I was going through the 'dark night of the soul' that almost invariably follows awakening. It lasted for years in one form or another. I was confused.

And I probably needed a dog to ground me.

The Conjuring Possum, the Fence-Jumping Social Worker and the Labrador who Learnt to Bark

Dogs have always added indispensable flavour to my life. Once life had become magical, dogs were added in surprising ways when I needed them.

For sixteen years Ruby, the red setter/retriever, had been a soulful, thoughtful and fun companion. She nannied my children and saw me through a divorce and a couple of house moves, one interstate. After she went there was a sad dogless gap in our lives.

Then shortly before Christmas, I was woken one night at three a.m. by a ruckus in the dining room. I grabbed my baseball bat, expecting to face a burglar. Instead I found a sweet possum sitting at the dining-table, looking as though it was waiting for Christmas dinner. A misadventure must have led it down the chimney. So I opened the sash window and made a trail of apple pieces out onto the deck. Then back to bed, assuming the possum would follow the apple trail and be gone by morning. The possum evidently had no such thoughts.

Come the morning he or she was neatly and furrily curled asleep on top of the high bookcase. Against all odds, the ornaments and books on the shelves were completely undamaged and the sleeping possum looked adorably cuddly. I restrained myself from stroking it, and instead phoned the RSPCA for advice. It was suggested that this might be a young male, who had been thrown out of the nest by its mother. A possum box for my garden was advised.

So off I went with my son to see the wildlife-carer in Hawthorn, who had such boxes. Minon's old Edwardian home had been turned into a shelter for all sorts of animals, and we were on our way out again, replete with possum box, when at the gate we met a woman with a dog. Simultaneously I fell in love with this beautiful tricolour small collie type, she jumped up at me beseechingly, and the woman said, "You don't want a dog do you?" My son and I looked at each other just once and said, "Yes!"

The possum, who had left by the time we returned, must surely have come to lead us to the dog. It turned out that someone had found this gorgeous puppy under a log in the country. She was very timid at first, and reluctant to exit the crate she had arrived in. Coaxing her did not work, so I bounced a tennis ball a metre or so away until her curiosity got the better of her. From that day on I had a ball fanatic on my hands.

What to name this beautiful creature? I opened a book of mythology randomly to find a page all about the Fianna – the band of warriors who guarded Ireland. So she was called Finny for short.

It took her many years to get over her fear of men and their boots. It also took her years to get over her gratitude to me for adopting her. After two years of her excessive and obvious gratitude, I sat her down one day and told her there was no need for more.

Finny was a wonderful dog – intelligent, beautiful, speedy, and full of fun and humour. Known as the local social worker, she used to jump my five foot fence and do the rounds of neighbours for a play. They all loved her and one kept a specially padded stick to throw for her. At first she slept outside in a kennel, until one day while out walking we met a young woman who enquired if this was my dog. I replied affirmatively and asked why.

"My father is a butcher," she explained. "Your dog comes to visit ours every night about midnight. They trot off down to the park together for a play, then they come back here, your dog takes a bone and off she goes." I had wondered about the source of all the mysterious bones in my garden.

That was the end of Finny's night-time exploits. She slept inside from then on. But the daytime fence jumping was still a worry. Within a week of buying a beautiful labradorite pendant, a friend phoned me to ask if I would find someone to take a labrador whose family was splitting up. I said I would. Maybe with a friend at home, Finny would stay home too.

Beau was already six, a big handsome golden retriever labrador cross. He was miserable about his broken family, who instructed me not to let him off the lead when walking. They also told me he had never barked. Soon after his adoption he was a changed character. He became very jolly, fell totally in love with me, goofed around in the park off the lead and found his voice. He took to having joyously loud, throaty conversations with me in the front garden, which must surely have been heard all around the block. In the house he would position himself in the passage, where he could follow my every move with his adoring gaze.

Three Important Questions and my Chocolate Lover from Across the Bay

After the tragic and sudden loss of Finny and Beau, there was a very long gap. For six years I was dogless and it didn't suit me. At the pier, the park and the beach I became an obsessive dog whisperer and patter. My daughter insistently dragged me to the RSPCA several times, but that is not how I came across Charlie.

Having surrendered to the fact that I was just not a whole person sans canine, I decided on a spoodle, and scoured Gumtree online for one already house-trained. After missing a few, eventually I found one not already taken, a chocolate miniature. I hopefully phoned Spiro, the owner, to find he lived near Ballarat, on the other side of Port Phillip Bay. He told me that two lots of would-be takers were coming to compete over the dog the following day.

I had clearly missed out and was ready to put down the phone, but the conversation continued.

"I adore this dog," Spiro said. "He is like a child to me. How am I going to decide who to give him to?" So I found myself counselling him on how to choose. Then I referred to one of the photos of the dog he had posted in his advertisement, where it was licking a chocolate-coated ice cream.

"Don't you realise chocolate is poison to dogs?" He didn't. Strangely, the conversation continued, and he explained this dog was 'one out of the box – very special.' I had my grandchildren coming to stay the next day and knew there was no way I could go near Ballarat for days.

Then Spiro said, "I am going to ask you three questions."

By now I was simply going with the flow. His first question was about the meaning of life. I told him this happened to be my favourite question, and gave him an answer I believed at the time. Then he asked what time I got up in the morning and how old I was. "By ten in the morning he wants to play, and I want him to go to the right person – someone over forty-five." The conversation continued until near 11 p.m., when he asked me if I wanted the dog. I replied that if the dog was as he described, then yes I did.

"Well," he said, "You enjoy your grandchildren and come up and get him when you're ready. I'm going to tell the others he's taken."

So that's how Charlie came to live with me – the curly, brown doggie love of my life, personal trainer, secretary, comedian, night watchman and couch hot water bottle – against all odds. It was clearly meant to be. After a few months, judging by the photos I sent him of Charlie in his new home, being cuddled by grandchildren, eyeing me from his bed or sitting on my office chair, Spiro happily declared the match 'a marriage made in heaven.'

My Dog Deserves a Salary

My dog deserves a salary
He does so many things for me
To look at him you wouldn't know
That he's the one who runs the show

To prevent my sad demise
He insists I exercise
Personal trainer is his role
Fulfilled with all his furry soul

He is my secretary too
At phone calls yelling "Yoo-hoo-hoo!"
When I'm outside this is a help
His tortured-sounding phone call yelp

At the Thermomix's sound
He calls more quietly I've found
When cold I needn't even ask
Hot water bottle is his task

Friendship and charm he so extends
That he has made me many friends
He has his fans at park and beach
Politely greeting all and each

But anyone behaving badly
Will not be tolerated gladly
Don't mess with me or be a clown
Or he will put his paw right down.

Meanwhile my feng shui work continued …

Unbearable Nights and a Delicious Breakfast

Nicky and David imported and sold beautiful Indonesian furniture in a suburb near mine. They were a warm, genuine and friendly couple, and I took to them and to their shop. After pottering there a while, I bought a lovely, curvaceous teak coffee table. We got talking and it turned out they were interested in Feng Shui, and were willing to kindly display my brochures in their shop. This led to my giving a feng shui talk there one evening, and a continued friendly association. They recommended my services to interested customers, and I recommended their furniture to my clients. David even designed some furniture specifically to fit feng shui specifications.

When they told me they were moving house a year or two later, I offered to do the feng shui for them.

So, on a cloudy December afternoon, I found myself outside a pretty little Edwardian brick house, with neat privet-edged beds of iceberg roses. Nicky showed me round, and I was as surprised as I often am at the speed with which newly moved-in occupants can claim a house as home. It was charming – smallish but spacious, and, unsurprisingly, impeccably furnished in Indonesian style. Beautiful, carved wooden panels adorned some of the white walls; a big, low teak table with silky purple cushions on a lovely burgundy Persian rug had pride of place in the lounge; and everywhere were tasteful antique wooden pieces, interesting lamps, and warm coloured floor rugs. The main living room opened out into a tranquil, private walled courtyard with a pleasantly trickling fountain, and greenery covering the walls.

There were no major problems. A large Buddha needed moving into the hall; the antique headboard on the bed was too tall and needed changing; and the magnetic field reading was a bit too high in the front part of the house. The house generally felt and certainly looked lovely, and I was pleased to think it would probably support Nicky and David well.

When I popped into the shop a few weeks later, with the remedies for the electro-magnetic field they had ordered, they invited me to their New Year's Eve-cum-house-warming party. They were enjoying living in the house and were gradually implementing the feng shui changes needed.

Due to interstate travel I was unable to attend the party, but popped in again to the shop after my return, to wish them a Happy New Year. Nicky asked if it was possible she had put the remedies for the electromagnetic field in the wrong place, as she had started to have anxiety attacks and palpitations at night. In fact, her nights were so unbearable lately, she dreaded going to bed. I was puzzled, and asked when this had started. The electromagnetic field cures could not induce this kind of response – all they did was neutralise the harmful effect of the magnetism on the body and its energy field.

I thought perhaps some kind of energy had been brought into the bedroom by a visitor on the night of the party. David was there, polishing an attractive rounded bookcase, and joined in the conversation. Together we tried to figure out what might have triggered the beginning of the problem. Nicky mentioned they now had a new antique headboard on the bed. It was lower than the old one, as recommended, and many people had commented favourably on it at the party. Something went 'click' in my head. I knew the headboard was the culprit. David told me it had been a room divider, and was made of teak panels. We decided that it warranted another visit by me, and they offered me Sunday breakfast.

At ten o'clock on a sunny Sunday morning, unbreakfasted, I walked through to the lovely living area, where David was making coffee. He mentioned that he, too, had had a few nightmares lately. I dumped my briefcase, then wandered back curiously to look in the bedroom. I didn't even have to enter the room. Just standing outside the door and looking at the headboard, I could feel myself being assailed by a sickeningly thick, unpleasant energy – something like a sinister black cloud.

As I stood there with eyes closed, tuning in to this energy, I could see and hear much squabbling and scolding, mainly by a stout middle-aged woman, but by others too. This beautifully carved screen had been a room divider in a very conflicted household, and had imported the conflict straight into Nicky and David's house and consciousness. The perspiration Nicky had found herself nightly bathed in, was probably one of the ways her body had been trying to rid itself of the foul energy of the headboard; and the anxiety was her body's way of warning her something was very wrong.

It was not difficult to clear the energy, and, having done so, I felt a lovely, heavenly energy coming in to replace it, which would surely make for very sweet dreams!

When I told Nicky and David about the conflict energy of the headboard, they laughed, looked at each other, and both said that explained why they had been squabbling lately. Nicky admitted she could hardly wait to go to bed, to see what would happen.

However, it being only about ten thirty in the morning, and the job done, we sat down, around the marble-topped table, to a delicious breakfast of sourdough bread, berry jam and white cheese; and luscious pastries with cinnamon and apple tea.

P.S. A phone call from Nicky the following day revealed that they had slept well, and a few months later she was delighted to find herself expecting their long- awaited first child.

CHAPTER 16

From Manhunt to the Infinite

A Confusing Conundrum and The End of the Manhunt

I wasn't going to write about this, as it still disturbs me slightly, but you will no doubt want to know what happened to my ongoing manhunt. So I will cover the bare bones of this part of the story.

When I first moved down near the sea I walked on the pier daily. It was a delightful novelty and the water of the bay was a different colour each time – silvers, golds, greens and blues. Seagulls flashed about after scraps of fish and chips, stood on the sand looking out to sea or bobbed like little grey and white boats. At full moon the huge silver ball would rise on one side while the startling reds, golds and pinks of the setting sun dazzled on the other.

One day on the pier I was accosted by a rather lurching disoriented-looking young man. There were several people around but he aimed straight for me.

"What day is it?" He asked.

I told him, "Monday."

"I seem to have lost a day," he said. "I thought it was Sunday."

Then he explained he had had an argument with his girlfriend and must have slept for twenty-four hours. He was pleasant-looking and didn't seem drunk or drugged, just rather odd. I wondered if he was okay and asked if he'd like to come over the road with me to get something to eat.

We sat outside at a restaurant and he told me his story. I don't now recall all the details, but one thing that stood out was his mention of his 'master'. He was working as a public servant and this 'master' was someone he was learning from. As was my wont, I did not ask what kind of master this was. I assumed qi gong or some such martial art.

This young man and I met once more for a coffee. He spoke about his work, the problems he saw in the world, and at one point said, "Maybe it could be arranged for you to meet my master sometime."

At that time I was settling into my new home and not looking for a man via online dating or any other way. Those other interesting men I had met had all been ones I had found online and approached. However, a few weeks after this meeting with the young man, someone from the online dating site approached me. After a short email correspondence and a phone call, we met near the pier. He had warned me he was so big that most people were afraid of him. I had no idea what that meant.

A short-lived and utterly confusing relationship followed. In person he was average size, but he was anything but average. When he told stories they seemed to get into my mind, as though I was there. I suspected he might be an NLP (neuro linguistic programming) master. At times I felt inexplicably happy when he was around. Once next to him, my frequency or energy seemed to rise as though going up in a lift. I was afraid I might explode if it went too far, and stopped the process. He told me he was able to give talks on any topic and had students.

One day, while coming home from grocery shopping, I distinctly felt a ring on my left ring finger. But there was no ring there. Am I going to marry this man, I wondered. Or am I meant to think this?

This strange man seemed very keen to talk about the dark side of life – all the things wrong with the world, and how he had been mistreated by his mother. I did not like the dark talk – it seemed the opposite of the elevation I felt at times. He also talked about extraterrestrials and the need for some of the DNA of the right people to be kept to populate other planets in future. He said he would turn me into the person I was destined to be. I wasn't so sure at all about that.

I tried to place this man, who told me he went by a couple of different names – one his stage name and the other his real name. One of my aims in moving had been to get away from the people interfering in my life in my last house. Was he one of them, wheedling his way into my life here? Was he the 'master' the young man had suggested I meet? He was exceedingly charismatic, but nothing added up.

He had all his possessions in his car as he had just come from Perth, on the other side of Australia. I had been communicating online with another, apparently brilliant but rather odd man in Perth, and that correspondence had just ended. Was this the same person? When asked, his response was, "There's only one of me."

The odd thing is he left me with a gift. I have a slate floor in part of the house and am sensitive to chemicals. I had bemoaned to him the fact that the slate was getting scratched and I couldn't use the chemical to give it a new coating.

I spent a day in Melbourne working, leaving him in my house. A few times he had alluded to me trusting him. *'Should I or shouldn't I?'* I thought. I was wanting to trust life more at that stage, but in the form of *this* weird man?

On my return I noticed that the slate floor looked as good as new! There was no chemical smell. I later asked him what he had used on it and his response was, "only water." However this was over a decade ago and each time I mop that floor it comes up like new again.

As he had left, he had said as an aside, "My master told me never to give a woman anything unless they have earned it." I had no idea if this meant I had earned something or I hadn't, as he took back the akubra he had given me! Or did it mean the floor will only come up like new when I take the trouble to mop it?

I hope I am not confusing you as much as I was confused, dear reader. There is some sense in all this from the point of view of Life. I was being confused out of my mind, shown I have no control of my life, and it is wisest to simply surrender and trust Life. Peter used to call confusion 'co-fusion'. It shakes the mind out of its fixed patterns and ultimately brings one closer to reality. I had a very strong mind, and probably needed very strong confusion!

'One should remain as a witness to whatever happens, adopting the attitude, 'Let whatever strange things that happen happen, let us see!' This should be one's practice. Nothing happens by accident in the divine scheme of things.'

– **Ramana Maharshi**

More than a Saint's Hug, and an Angel or a Devil?

After it ended, my suspicions about this man increased and the etheric night time interference became worse. There were regularly noises from invisible night visitors and they were trying to interact with me. In fact this was when the slashed hot water bottle event happened.

Another odd incident at that time was a visit with thousands of others to Amma, the hugging saint. People queued up, were given a hug from Amma and moved on. When I reached the front of the queue, Amma spoke to her offsider and he stroked my back. Then she made a marking on my forehead prior to the hug. No-one else in the queue was getting either a backrub or a marking. There was no way I could find out what that was all about. Did she know I was being psychically attacked? Was this some kind of protection?

Many years later I still tried to categorize this man as angel or devil, but could not. I was so puzzled when I knew him that I repeatedly consulted the tarot on him, and each time the devil card came up. This of course does not mean he was a devil, but can have some dubious connotations, including a connection with the occult. Interestingly, during the short time of interacting I had a strong intuitive knowing that my assessment of him would be exactly what I received. I had suspected he was evil, so apparently evil is what I got.

> Do not ever jump to conclusions, which means: don't judge. You cannot see properly, so how are you qualified to judge? You may see the light and the dark, but see it all as light, for it is ultimately. It must be, as there is nothing else. You do not believe the actor in the movie, playing the villain, is a real villain. So it is in life. Nothing is as it seems. It is all light. How can you judge light by its reflections? That is insanity!

He told me I would soon meet someone else, and indeed soon after that a rather creepy man approached me on the pier. He got short shrift, but kept appearing for a while, to no avail. However, at the same time I also met a friendly young woman who pointed me to numerous helpful delights in my new area. Together we joined a weekend of soul-dancing in a beautiful forest- lined centre nearby, and attended other healing groups in lovely venues, which I would never have found. After a couple of months she disappeared. Her coming and going in my life was as mysterious as anything else. I did wonder if she was one of his pupils, appointed to cheer me up after my discombobulating time with him.

As a result of the domestic violence he had endured at the hands of his mother when a child, and later at the hands of his wife, he had told me his mission now was to attend to the domestic violence in this country. When I asked how he could do that, he replied that he 'had ways'.

A few months after he had told me this, a tragic event took place in a suburb not far from mine. A beautiful eleven year old boy was brutally killed by his mentally ill father at a cricket practice, in front of horrified onlookers. The effect of this tragedy was to bring the conversation about domestic violence into the forefront of the whole country at last.

The boy's mother, grief stricken at the loss of her only child, but also intelligent and courageous, worked to bring this huge and largely ignored problem to light, and later became Australian of the Year. The problem in this country is by no means fixed, but at least it is recognized, and more help for victims has been set up.

Behind the scenes of our lives there are those powerful enough to quietly steer events, as the Masters of the Far East apparently do. I wondered if that man I had met was one of them. Or if he was an extraterrestrial.

You had some experiences that shook you right out of your belief systems. Since then you do not know what to believe. It is best to keep it that way. Keep beliefs to a minimum and trust and faith to a maximum. Instead what you have been doing is scrabbling around trying to gather evidence to create new beliefs that you can hold onto. But this is not life's plan for you. So it does not work. Know you are not your beliefs. What you are is the same as these men. You ARE. And all the time you spend trying to formulate beliefs and control is time wasted from awareness of what you really are. Pretend you are nothing and no-one and go from there. That would be better than any identity. You are a hollow tube through which life lives.

The mind may not be where truth lies, but it is a filter through which your responses happen. If this filter is clogged with untruth your responses will be odd and inappropriate. So the more clarity you can install in the mind, the more the inner can express clearly and undilutedly.

The effect of this little brush with the unknown in the form of an enigmatic man was to put me off trying to seek any male partner. If a suitable one came along, fine. If not, so be it. With hindsight, this whole manhunt was a wilful detour – a fruitful one, but a detour nonetheless. I had felt sure that I needed to have a successful long term relationship with a man, as part of my journey in this life.

My marriage lasted fourteen years and gave us some good times and two wonderful children, but was fraught with immaturity and incompatibility. We get on well now in our older years, but being from very different families, had very different values and tastes. After our divorce I had been happily on my own for over a decade before the three year manhunt began.

A second reason to wish for a relationship was the sinister aspect that had crept into my life and the need for protection. It was never the usual bedtime exploits that attracted me – I had already by then had transcendent experiences that so far exceeded what they could offer.

Many years before, I had run a spiritual development course for teenagers. One of them, who was very psychic, told me my soulmate was not alive at this time. So I wasn't after a soulmate, just someone compatible and a relationship of mutual growth. But Life obviously had other plans for me.

Soon after deciding to stop looking, my male partner rocked up in the form of Charlie, the friendly, curly, uncomplicated spoodle!

> The fewer parameters you specify for your happiness, the more life can satisfy you. If you are kind to life and let it flow as it wishes, it will be kind to you.

Marvelous Monks and Sand Mandalas

I discovered some interesting spiritual offerings in my new beachside location.

Only a few streets away was a zendo at the back of a house. The owner was an Australian builder and monk who had trained at a Zen monastery in Japan and had been given the Abbott's blessing to start his own zendo, which had been properly consecrated. A friend and I decided to go there and meditate daily from 6 - 7 seven a.m. with Paul for a year.

We would enter silently and sit on cushions, eyes open, facing the wall, simply observing the mind. This would be alternated with walking meditation. Paul would ring the bell to begin and end the meditation, and when it was all over we would go in and have a rice porridge breakfast with him. I found this practice very powerful, and it was much easier to meditate there than at home. I recall one walking meditation with tears streaming down my cheeks. I had no idea why, or if they were my tears or the world's.

The other interesting local treasure was the annual visit of the Tibetan monks, now living in India. They were usually a group of about eight young men, with one venerable older lama. (A Tibetan lama is a highly accomplished teacher of Tibetan Buddhism). Several of these monks had escaped Tibet after the Chinese had invaded. Wearing their traditional Buddhist robes of maroon and gold they would smilingly lead activities with children, and rituals with adults.

During the days they spent here, they would create extraordinarily intricate and colourful sand mandalas, from memory, blowing the sand delicately into position through straws. On the final night they would ceremoniously sweep away the sand and give little bags of it, with the colours all mixed up, to those present. Their care and the subsequent destruction of their creation was illustrative of the impermanence of life, and the consequent need for detachment.

The old lama gave talks which were interpreted by a humorous and lively Tibetan, who also manned the stall where many different items were sold to help fund the tour. Here one could buy prayer flags, jewellery of semi-precious stones, singing bowls, beautiful woollen rugs and Tibetan wall hangings and paintings. Then one could take the purchase to a monk for a blessing.

These monks seemed very happy, regardless of their country's devastating invasion, and the traumatic escapes many had survived. Their training was very rigorous. Starting at a young age, they had to memorize a tremendous amount, including the long guttural chants we heard them perform.

There were many memorable New Year's Eve concerts with a shakuhachi flute player and the monks chanting in all their finery, ending in a walk to the candle-lit beach and further chants, before we watched fireworks exploding all around the bay.

Orbs on the beach at New Year's Eve, with the Tibetan monks in their finery.

On one such night I took photographs, and was surprised to find the dark air full of orbs of light in the pictures. It seemed numerous spirits had come to join the celebration!

The old lama was the only one who returned year after year. For the young monks touring much of Australia was an adventure and a holiday. These tours stopped a few years ago, due perhaps to tiredness on the part of the woman who had kindly and efficiently organised them for so many years.

Meanwhile my channeling often told me simply to 'be still'.

Quietness

Quietness is a gift.

Quietness is a sanctuary within which peace and recognition reside.

Quietness is respite from the busy outer world. Our souls and true nature may be found within its deep recesses.

Quietness holds all solutions. All inventions arise from it.

Quietness is the compass of integrity.

Within quietness, all knowledge may be accessed.

When quietness is lost, so is wisdom.

Absolute quietness is a space, which automatically becomes filled with universal truth.

Seek absolute quietness and you will gain wisdom

'I think 99 times and find nothing. I stop thinking, swim in silence, and the truth comes to me.'

– Albert Einstein

Swapping Places with Infinity

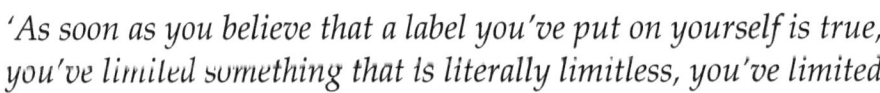

'As soon as you believe that a label you've put on yourself is true, you've limited something that is literally limitless, you've limited who you are into nothing but a thought.'

– Adyashanti

Maybe it was the monks, maybe it was meditation, timing or grace, but one day in 2010 I swapped places with infinity.

It is impossible to describe or explain these sorts of experiences. The best I can do is to say I identified as totally boundless and was aware that somewhere within this infinity of myself, there was a tiny form called Paula. I had no idea what she was doing there – she was like a sort of blot on perfection. This sense of being infinity itself went on for days. It is a mystery to me how I functioned, but I did. I now suppose that is due to the fact that it was not 'I' that functioned, but Life itself, functioning as always through this Paula-form.

My channeling now often took the form of a sort of diary:

On the beach the other day I felt so expansive that I was everything. I am noticing strange things happening. Last night I was at the hot springs and said to someone (under the overcast sky) that I'd love the stars to be out. Within a short time they were all out and the sky was clear. It all seems magical. And other things seem to happen by themselves. E.g. the inside car light came on before I went to it, my paper was brought in while I was out. I don't understand it but it's nice. At the market a man appeared out of the blue and helped me with my bags. Today I feel so happy and as though the real me is a dancing, carefree, weightless diva, who must animate this dense body-mind.

After that experience faded, as with the others, it left its flavour in my mind, and a greater space of possibility. That sense of the infinite remains as the backdrop to my days.

Squeeze me into another day

Squeeze me into another day
O Lord - whoever you are -
Squeeze me this day again
Into form
That I may do the will of
Whoever's will I do

While I prefer to fly formless
In the vacant arms of Infinity
I shall shape myself this day
Into form again
And see
What happens here.

'For when you see that the universe cannot be distinguished from how you act upon it, there is neither fate nor free will, self nor other. There is simply one all-inclusive Happening, in which your personal sensation of being alive occurs in just the same way as the river flowing and the stars shining far out in space. There is no question of submitting or accepting or going with it, for what happens in and as you is no different from what happens as it.'

– Alan Watts

The profound experiences I had, had changed my mind. I noticed I was far more dispassionate and detached than before. The tips of the waves of my mind might ruffle, but that ruffle did not go very deep or linger very long. I watched the news as if watching a movie, feeling compassion but not getting swamped by it as I might have before. There was a sense of timelessness and a trust in life. Things would happen as they had to happen and all would ultimately work out. I now understood my father's 'all is well', and I was very grateful for my life, even if I could neither understand nor control it.

Another effect was that the three dimensional world of forms and the five senses – the phenomenal world – no longer impressed me so much. Whereas in the past I had revelled in the beauty and richness of the five senses, I had now tasted something so far superior as to be incomparable, in the transcendent. The ecstasy I had felt could not be conjured up by any mundane if enjoyable experience.

> Your world must have form. It is like the backbone which spirit leans upon to express itself.
>
> You do not need to force structure into your life. It will happen regardless of what you decide to do or not do. Life automatically produces structure. Because life is form and form is actually a structure - visible or invisible. Where there is life there will be structure.

Sitting on a bench near the local pier one day, an intelligent looking man about my age asked permission to join me. Once seated, as we both gazed at the sparkling blue water reflecting the sunlight, his opening line was, rather strangely, "You wouldn't be dead for quids, would you?"

My response was, "I don't know… I am rather looking forward to the afterlife…"

Of course I had no intention of summoning the afterlife ahead of time, but the idea of that freedom from forms and restriction was a delightful prospect. It took years for me to integrate the life of form and formless in a more satisfactory way.

> The reality is so much bigger than anything you can possibly see from your mind and senses. To base your ideas and actions on these is to be out of touch with the real. The real is alive, flowing, juicy and perfect. It will fulfill your deepest needs first, always. Your mind, on the other hand, has little knowledge of your deepest needs. It only knows of your superficial desires and fears. You may be kept busy listening to these all your life. But eventually you will tire of this, as it seems so fruitless ultimately.

CHAPTER 17

A New Challenge and Taking Stock

Holographic Hum and a Big Challenge

Let life flow through your fingers like sand at the beach. Do not hang onto any part of it. That way you remain as the unchanging.

Throughout all these years I continued to sit at my computer with my intuitive writing/channeling. Sometimes I would have questions and listen for the answers. Other times I might just see if information wanted to come through. During the earlier years much information came through, but later it was generally only in response to my questions. And later still I had fewer and fewer questions, and did less and less writing. When unsure if I was making up the answer or getting it wrong, I would check the accuracy with my dowsing rod, which was reliable for this.

Perhaps this channeled piece explained some of the remarkable things I had seen my wide-awake friends do.

So the chair upon which you sit is alive. It is moving, it is feeling, it is, in a sense, breathing, in that it is constantly exchanging energy with its environment. Everything around you, in your home, in your garden, in your work-place, is alive. There is no dead piece of cardboard or sleeping rock. Everything hums. And that hum affects you, the humans, in the midst of it. This is profoundly important to you. The quality of the hum or vibration dictates your own, to a large extent, because it is in constant exchange with you. Remember, there are no boundaries in reality - everything is linked. This link is not just slight as in the linear links of a chain. It is complete, as in a hologram. Until you learn to create your own frequency, independent of your environment, you will be an interdependent part of the hologram. You are able to learn to create your own tune, because of your unique link to your creator. If you make the link to your creator stronger than your link to the material world, this will override the surrounding vibratory effect. You will then be able to transmit your own frequency into the world, without being affected by it. This is a position of great power.

This must be how Peter had chain-smoked all his adult life and swallowed poison accidentally without ill effect. Sadly, it seemed I was not yet in that place of great power, as the environmental hum around me, in the form of the radiation involved in telecommunications and smart meters, was starting to affect me adversely.

After installing solar panels in 2009, my electricity meter was replaced with a so-called 'smart' meter. These meters, maybe not really so smart, transmit information via radio frequency radiation. Soon after that I could not think straight, could not make decisions, was emotional, fatigued and had palpitations. It took me a while to work out that my body was reacting to the radiation from the meter.

Mobile phone technology went from 2G to 3G to 4G, and with each increase of transmission from the phone towers my body suffered, and I had to find ways to be able to function and to sleep. I could not use a cell phone due to this, nor could I spend time with people using their phones. If I was standing in a queue and the person next to me took out her phone, I would have to escape, forfeiting my place in the queue.

As this technology became more widespread and the frequencies departed further from our natural frequencies, more people across the globe became affected as I was. Websites with research and advice sprang up, building biologists learnt about ways to help people, and products such as shielding clothing became available, if costly. I could use a computer and landline as long as everything was hardwired and wifi was disabled. Shielding on my head was a lifesaver. I spent thousands of dollars on all sorts of gadgets and therapies that either did not work, or only worked for a short time.

Ladi, my trusted naturopath, was now far from where I lived and was aging. A visiting doctor from Tasmania, who had added alternative methods to her repertoire, helped. Using muscle testing she found Ashwaganda, an adaptogenic herb, would energise me, and it did. But nothing seemed enough to get me back to normal, and the telecommunications industry kept upping the frequencies. I had to find ways to survive the radiation onslaught, and much of my time, attention and finances was spent to that end. This was another reason for my manhunt to end – my life was surely now too complicated for anyone else to deal with.

Initially I was still running my feng shui business, and although I enjoyed it, there were some problems. I was now living an hour from Melbourne, and most of my clients were around that area, some being two hours or more from my new home.

Then, due to my spiritual adventures, I now had the idea that concepts were not such a good idea – that perhaps I was limiting my clients by putting concepts about feng shui into their heads. I had seen that the concepts we all share are like a house of cards, built on nothing except belief. If anything was possible, and we are all made of power, surely I should not be encircling my clients with a model of do's and don'ts – with ideas of feng shui problems that they might unknowingly activate? In retrospect this seems rather silly, but I was determined to do no harm. I discussed my concerns with several clients, who all assured me that I was helping and should continue.

> *'To expound and propagate concepts is simple, to drop all concepts is difficult and rare.'*
> **– Sri Nisargadatta Maharaj**

Then the third factor was this new problem with mobile phones and wifi. Clients would obligingly turn their wifi off for me, but would forget about their teenagers' cell phones or their spouses' ipads. Then my head would reel, my heart would race, I would feel like crying and I couldn't think. Many businesses relied on their wifi and had to leave it on.

In addition to all that, the words of the palm reader in Bangkok rang in my ears. He had told me that I could work with ghosts and entities, but must stop when I am old, or I might get sick. Well I already had health problems. Would dealing with entities or tainted energy worsen them? All in all it just became unworkable for me to continue. I wrote a 'thank you and goodbye' email to my many clients, and gave my still flourishing business away.

> You will never be forced to make a decision. Decisions make themselves.
>
> How so?
>
> Decisions, like fears or arguments, are entities. They are a frequency and a consciousness. The possibilities of decision are already there, waiting to be activated by agreement. When an agreement happens - a like frequency - the decision comes into force, or you might say, into play. No individual has ever 'made a decision.'
>
> This is a surprise! Can you tell me more about this please? How does it then seem as if we do?
>
> It seems this way, as you see the result of the decision and seek a cause. Man has an over-inflated view of his effect in this world. He automatically believes he must be the cause of the decision which has come into play.
>
> Is this not because his thoughts seemed to lead to it?
>
> Yes it might seem this way. But in fact the thoughts are part of the decision itself.
>
> They are, in a sense, the introduction to the decision. When the frequency of the situation is right, the thoughts and the decision are made. Nothing can stop them at this point. They are birthed just as a child is.

So if, in my life I do not seem to be making decisions, this is not a problem - the time is just not right for them to be made.

Exactly.

And if the time was right I could not stop them being made.

Yes.

So I really can relax and watch my life being played.

What you feel pressed to do you will do. What your mind mulls over and worries about, these are best ignored. They are circular.

Greek Delicacies, a Police Escort, the Swedish Palace and Serendipity

It had never been my plan to retire and spend my days playing tennis or bridge. I had always assumed I would be feng shui consulting until I was seventy-four, for some unknown reason! But necessity had stolen my feng shui career from me long before that. I hoped a third career would materialize somehow, as magically as the last one had. Meanwhile I had more time to look at the world, inner and outer.

I looked back at my life and realized how extraordinarily well I had been looked after. Time and again I could have encountered disaster but had not. Apart from the large factors like living in a benign, peaceful country, growing up in a fairly wise family, and now having a kind, intelligent and ethical family of my own, even including a caring former husband, in so many little ways I had been fortunate.

As a child, my father often used to put his hand on my head and affectionately say, "Bless you". Maybe these blessings piled up and affected my life more than I knew.

Years ago a friend remarked that I was very good at manifesting food. For eighteen years I lived opposite Jim, a kind Greek man who grew his own vegetables and was forever surprising me with little fruit and vegetable gifts. My letter box would be stuffed with zucchinis, there would be a capsicum on my car bonnet, or baked Greek delicacies from his wife at Easter. Joan, a local friend, would often leave cooked meals at my front door. Some of the restaurateurs I worked for insisted on serving me meals. At one farm I attended where money was short, I was paid in fresh eggs, garlic ropes and other produce.

This was part of a letter written to my mother in about 2000:

'I cannot get over how well I am looked after! People seem to give me presents daily. Yesterday Finny and I managed to lose her ball in the park. The very same day (without me saying anything about that) Jim gave Finny a new ball, gave me a huge cucumber, a bag of nectarines and a bunch of dahlias. Today a friend left a CD she had copied for me on the doorstep, and another friend gave me a lovely shawl and a box of rice chips (her husband works for the company that make them). Two days ago she gave me two more boxes of these and two dips she had made, and a delicious piece of date and chocolate torte. It goes on like this day after day! I almost expect something on the doorstep when I get home! Jim hangs bags of fruit and vegies as a surprise on my gate for me – recently tomatoes, plums, nectarines, cucumbers. If I tell him I have enough he still gives them to me and says to give them to my friends!

I even had the police looking after me the other day. I was on my way to a job at a function centre where a big bar mitzvah is going to be held for a wealthy client of mine who spares no expense. She wanted me to come – months ahead of time – and give advice on where the band, speeches, etc. should be positioned. This function centre was in a very difficult place to find, on a wharf at the docks near the city, but I used the map to figure out exactly how to get there, and was sure I had it taped! It was on South Wharf Road. I followed the map to the letter I thought, and found myself hopelessly lost. Seeing a sign for North Wharf Road in the distance I aimed for that, thinking perhaps from there I could find the south one. However then I couldn't find an exit from the North one and my problems compounded. I was by then quite late. Suddenly a police car appeared. I stopped them, wound down my window, told them I was lost, and asked if they knew how to get to South Wharf Road. They were most helpful, and after giving me numerous directions, suggested it would be quicker if they drove there and I followed! So I had a police escort to my job! No wonder I had got lost – it was basically in a car park, and I had gone right past it! Luckily my client got even more lost than I did, with no police escort, and arrived there ten minutes after me!'

Then there was the time I was overseas, and interstate friends were looking after my house and dogs. A dramatic storm resulted in a couple of large branches falling from one of my trees. These branches could have wreaked havoc on the garden, house and other structures. Instead they had carefully fallen into a position where they broke guttering and fencing that needed replacing anyway, while not damaging anything in the garden! The poor house-sitters had to deal with the practicalities, and insurance paid for much-needed replacements of guttering and fence.

One day I worked until very late and was worried about my dogs being alone for so long. However on my return I found my son had visited, bringing the dogs a new toy, and had played with them in my absence. How did that happen exactly on the day it was needed?

Throughout my life people seemed to show up when I needed them. I took my children away camping when they were still young, and there found another single mother with her children. She had sensed she would meet someone. To our surprise, we discovered we lived about two kilometers apart and became close friends for twenty years. The ups and downs of single parenting were shared and the hard times were diluted with fun. There were many giggles over advertisements in dating magazines, before the days of online dating sites. We discovered that we both liked apple pies and, oddly, surprised each other on the very same day with one in each others' letter boxes!

At the start of my feng shui career I was fortunate to have clients with large networks, who referred numerous friends or clients to me. My clients' word of mouth kept my business going and many of them became valued friends.

Then there were the 'cherry on the cake' moments which often happened on my travels. So often I happened to be in a country at the right moment to join in an unexpected celebration. In Stockholm I saw the royal family and toured the palace as there was a special holiday and free palace entry. At Esalen there was that extraordinary concert by Joan Baez – unannounced beforehand. In England my daughter and I had been having breakfast at a B and B, and struck up a conversation with a friendly woman at a nearby table. We ended up spending the night at her Cornwall seaside home. Also in England, one of our neighbours from my early childhood in Cape Town was a guide at one of the grand stately homes, and gave us a private tour after hours. We were breath-taken by the lavish gilded ceilings, furnishings and art, then spent the night at her pretty thatched country cottage. This list of serendipity could go on and on.

It has been said that if we believe we are separate individuals, we have to look after ourselves, but if we know we are one with everything, everything looks after us. This seems common sense. If we believe we have to look after ourselves we tend to try to control things, which does not always enable life to flow our best options to us. Whereas when we know we are one with everything and are never alone, we tend to relax, trust life and flow where it takes us. I cannot say I have been particularly relaxed or trusting, but perhaps just the knowing of the unity of life has helped my good fortune.

So many across the world are enduring terrible suffering or hardship, and I am reminded of a consultant psychiatrist I used to work with in South Africa. We were having a case conference about a professional man, who had six children and a sound marriage, but was so unspeakably sad that tears streamed down his frozen face all day, for no known reason.

"There but for the grace of God go I", murmured the compassionate psychiatrist.

I am so grateful for my life.

Of course, like everyone, I had dark times – homesickness, grief, worry, anger, regret, sickness, fear and confusion. But the good fortune far outweighed the bad, in retrospect. It was as though there was always a golden thread running through even the worst of times.

This reminds me of an attractive client I had, who had been in Port Arthur, Tasmania, with her young son on the day of the massacre by a lone gunman in 1996. He killed thirty-five people, wounded twenty-three others and caused Australia's current strong gun laws.

Lindal, my client, had been shot in the arm and ran to hide, desperate to protect her little boy. They sat on a step around the corner from the shooter, praying to be spared. On either side of them she saw a small angel sitting with them. Then she knew they would be alright. Perhaps the trauma of the moment had made her clairvoyant. I am sure these light beings are around us at all times, eager to help where they can. Being quiet and listening to our intuition helps them to help us.

I saw not only my good fortune, but the intricate webs that must be woven by Life in the time and space of our lives, for these events to take place. It is harder to believe that these events happen randomly, than that they are somehow orchestrated by an intelligence so far exceeding ours as to make it utterly incomprehensible.

'Life sustains itself. Let go of the ego and life takes care of itself through you.'

– Adyashanti

Department Stores, Slavery, Opshops and Righteous Indignation

It is the time for beings to focus inwards instead of outwards. It is what is on the inside which creates the world, not what is on the outside. The visible is merely the symptom of the invisible. So to learn how to work with the invisible is the task at hand.

Nevertheless, looking at the outer world, I was concerned at what I saw. Without my feng shui work, I became more aware of our societal problems and injustices, and the extent of their effect upon our environment. And I developed a distaste for department store shopping with its ridiculously cheap prices, so often due to virtual slave labour overseas; and its apparent disregard for the preciousness of the planet's resources. Opportunity shops became my preferred source of clothing.

Clearance Sale

Huge clearance! Demo models too!
Come buy it cheap today!
Don't worry - it won't cost you much
The Earth will have to pay

The metal comes from underground
The oil for plastic too
And there's plenty more around
For stuff for me and you

Don't hesitate to spend your cash
Though Earth is crying out
Container ships from overseas
Are circling all about.

Junk Mail

What's in the catalogue today
And how much will I have to pay?
It looks so cheap I might buy two -
One for me and one for you.

I'm looking at the printed cost
But ask
What else might I have lost?

There's fifty dollars to the shop
And my integrity will drop
For subsidizing slavery
Somewhere across an unknown sea.

And then the ugly sense of greed
For raping Earth more than I need;
Plus transport costs are not a minor
As we import it all from China

Take all that into account
And I'd be paying no small amount
So I will keep my fifty bucks
And rather go and watch the ducks

I resisted buying down-filled products unless they were cruelty free, looked askance at others buying cage eggs, and donated to Animals Australia, who do a wonderful job of standing up for species who cannot advocate for themselves. I found out more about agribusiness and was horrified at the whitewashed treatment of animals eaten so casually, after being treated so cruelly in a secretive industry geared only to make money, at the expense of the rights of other sentient beings. I became rather an expert at righteous indignation on many fronts!

> The appearance of the world is but a mirror. Changing the image does not change the origin. The image will change as the origin changes.
>
> Everything that happens is an equal and opposite reaction to everything else. To try to fix it is to continue the reverberation. The way to peace is acceptance and gratitude. This takes it back to neutral – the point of origination and the creativity of the new.
>
> All attempts to fix keep the original situation/ perceived problem alive – albeit in altered form. The only way out is forgiveness, acceptance, gratitude, receptive perception.
>
> Any attempt to heal which views anything as a problem merely chases the reverberation into another form.
>
> Its larger effect will be to increase comparison and suffering, through increasing individual will and goals. Peace lies at the fulcrum. When I am pro or anti I am making reverberations. When I'm the fulcrum I'm allowing peace.

If I try to save the world I'll create an equal and opposite response. So the more light workers, the more dark workers and vice versa. If we want peace we must be peace.

How on earth to integrate all that when there was so much that seemed so wrong? Surely we have to DO something?

Peace, Power and Protests

'Your duty is to Be, and not to be this or that.'
– Ramana Maharshi

Daily I wondered what on earth I was doing now, with no apparent purpose, no mission to fulfil. For the first time in my adult life I was just 'here', and I had so many judgements and ideas about that! Dark chocolate was employed to mask my dark thoughts.

It's just so hard to totally give up the notion of some goal or other... I feel suspended in the dark. Just dangling. Nothing in front of me and nothing behind. Nothing either side. In a mental and emotional void. What do you do with will when you have nothing to direct it to?

Direct it into every single thing you do or think. Choose your thoughts and actions very carefully then, as each will hold much power.

Trust in the moment. It is sufficient unto itself. Nothing need be added. Do you not think the whole universe is on your side? Allow it to carry you to your destination. Do not waste energy kicking and screaming and telling it where to go. Allow it to do all the work. Your part is merely to nod assent and go with the flow. It is the easiest part possible, provided you create no expectations or comparisons.

So the way my head hurts when I effort or think - is that there as a clue for me - reminding me when I am getting it wrong?

You could say this. It is a reminder that when you try to control events you are hitting your head against a wall. Whereas when you merely slow down and listen to the quiet directing voice inside, you can experience lightness of being and magic in your life.

On reflection, this time provided the opportunity to begin to integrate the spiritual experiences I had had, which had left me quite confused about relative and absolute; the mundane and the sublime. How to live the relative life of polarities, while having seen beyond them?

I had plenty of time to contemplate and also to channel information. What I didn't have at that stage was peace. There were glimpses of being present, but there was still the inner leaning forward into the future – looking for a cause, rather than simply being. I was so used to *doing*, that *being* somehow felt not enough, although I knew it was just what I and the planet needed.

'As muddy water is best cleared by leaving it alone, it could be argued that those who sit quietly and do nothing are making one of the best possible contributions to a world in turmoil.'
– Alan Watts

One cannot make peace with another while one is at war with oneself. While fifty people demonstrate against a war or a policy, one can quietly stay at home and be totally at peace, and that one will have more effect than the fifty. Why? Because they are not at peace, therefore have little of their power behind them. Noise does not equate with power. Power is what you all intrinsically are. Therefore the closer you can be to what you really are, the more power you will have. Essentially you are peaceful and loving. The more you can feel that, the more of your power you have access to.

What happens in the world is the eventual result of thought. Thoughts create pathways and actions within those pathways. Thoughts created by those out of sync with who they really are not as powerful as those created by people aware of their peace and their love. If ten really aware and awake people were to imagine a peaceful and just world, and make the smallest move towards this, they would have an enormous effect. Millions of people may want peace, but if they do not carry it in their hearts their desire will have little effect. And if they turn their desire into a protest against war, it will in fact have to be mirrored by an increase in protest.

Peace begets peace, protest begets protest. It is just fortunate that those who protest have little power, even in great numbers! Eventually sometimes if protests are ugly enough and persevering enough, they may change a system, through fear. Ideally this is not the best way to create change, as the world does not need more fear. It needs more love. We do not mean you to love that which you oppose. But love and be peaceful generally. Let your peace spread around and it will be having far more effect than you realise. Do not be misled into thinking only that which is visible or audible has effect. That has never been so, and it is in fact less true now than ever.

Peace has no antidote and no opposite. The opposite of war is understanding. Peace is the baseline.

Maybe I was channeling Mahatma Ghandi? His peace seemed to have dissolved colonialism in India – that was no mean feat!

Supermarkets, Seeds and Sugar-gliders

Habits die hard, so I took on causes, one after the other, in order to feel I was earning my keep. I attended some sustainability workshops, which fired me up for action. As well as trying to grow my own fruit and vegetables at home, I became a volunteer gardener at a local historic homestead, The Briars.

Here, under the expert guidance of a horticulturist and farmer, a small team of us turned a field into an edible garden in the style of the 1850's. This was the era of the homestead, which had surprising historical links with Napoleon Bonaparte. In the early 1800's, William Balcombe and his family lived on St Helena as did the exiled Napoleon. They became friends, with Napoleon subsequently giving the family many gifts. Some of these items were later housed at the Briars, which had been the home of Alexander, the youngest son of William Balcombe.

The aim of the garden was to preserve and distribute heritage seeds, fast disappearing due to multinational companies, monoculture, and globalization. The commercially available varieties of most fruits and vegetables have greatly decreased over the past century. Consumers expect the range of produce to be available no matter what the season, so it must be transported across the globe. Supermarkets want varieties which will ship and stack well without bruising, and will store well for months in cool rooms. Hence much store bought produce is now hard and tasteless. Large farms tend to follow monoculture practices, which cause pests and disease to thrive, and give rise to the use of pesticides, herbicides and genetic modification of crops.

Across the world there are now seed banks, due to the realization that we are losing precious species and need to save the varieties we still have. They also serve to prepare for possible disasters. The largest of these seed banks is the Svarlbard Global Seed Vault in the Arctic Circle, also known as the Doomsday Vault. Here the world's most diverse collection of seeds is safeguarded – now well over a million varieties.

We volunteers dug, planted, weeded, learnt how to make garlic plaits and compost tea, and save different kinds of seeds. Our efforts were punctuated by a sociable teabreak, various fat hens and a bossy rooster.

Enthused about sustainability, I decided to start the first food swap on my peninsula. The idea is that people bring their excess organically grown home harvest – fruit, vegetables, seedlings, honey, preserves, etc. – and take home someone else's. A crucial part is that no money is exchanged. It is all about abundance, generosity and community-building.

Happily, these food swaps operate commonly in many countries now, reducing in a small way, the need for food to be flown across the world, and encouraging community, edible home gardening and seasonal consumption.

Home Harvest Exchange

David Suzuki tells us
We are the chlorophyll
Made from the fire
Of the sun
And the breath of air
From the plant
Risen from the earth
And drunk on water
Eaten by the animal
That feeds our blood.

Jean Houston tells us
We are cloned from sunspots
United with light
Formed by the metabolism
Of the galaxy
Solar beings yet of the sea
Beaten by the rhythms
Of ocean and wave
And longing to remember

Our supermarkets tell us
We have credit cards
And notes in our purses
And need relieving
Of this burden
They tell us what's on special
So we can feel we are cheating
The system that
Is cheating us

Their lurid colours
Dazzle our eyes
And blur the small print
On the box

The Fresh Food aisles tell us
Our fruit is well-travelled
And experienced
Distant lands
Ships, planes and cold rooms
Radiation, spray and wax
We like no blemishes
Safe and shiny
Clean as clean can be
Fresh as yesterday
So we'll reach in that purse
And happily pay

Home Harvest Exchange tells us
We are part of something
Organic and wholesome
Friendly and fruitful
Local and lucky
Non-numerical
That the spiral of life
Is free and
Unerringly inclusive
If allowed to be
And that seeds
Can nurture both snails
And stars

I also volunteered for a local wildlife carer, an extraordinary woman, who had dedicated her life to caring for injured or neglected wild creatures. She regularly went to the shops with three bumps on her chest instead of two – the third being a baby possum or tiny joey in her tee shirt. Her house was a maze of outdoor and indoor cages and aviaries, and usually there would be a joey leaping around somewhere. My job was mostly cleaning cages and feeding all sorts of wonderful furry or feathered beings – from tawny frogmouths to sugar gliders to pelicans.

At the same time, I attended meetings about starting a community garden in my area, which eventually took off. We had to be granted land by the council and have the soil tested for contaminants. Then we involved the hardware store, mens' shed and Rotary club for supplies and building of beds and shelter. Our friend, the capable ranger from the homestead, designed a permaculture garden for us, and the planting began, at which point I confess to opting out, as my own garden and my electrosensitivity were demanding much of me.

CHAPTER 18

Resisting Being

Frustrating Frequencies and Maybe-Not-So-Smart Phones

While all this sustainability was enjoyable and took up some of my time, I knew it was not my real passion. And eventually Life stepped in again and said, "No, my friend, you will no longer distract yourself with this."

Really, I had been warned about how this works in 1999 by channeled information:

> Doing and being are equally needed in your world for balance. One is outward and linear, the other inward and cyclical. Yang and yin. Compare not the swallow to the ass – they both have their place!
>
> There is within you some struggle for supremacy. The part of you that seeks to achieve at times overrides the needs of the part that needs rest and quietness, and at other times the opposite is true (but less often.) These times seem to you to be dictated by what

you have to do. However that is not really the case. They are dictated by what is happening inside you at a soul level. For your soul gets into states of imbalance too, and needs rebalancing.

When you are tired, your soul will be inviting you to rest, your body will be giving you messages, and if you do not listen to either, eventually your environment will set it up for you. The circumstances in your life are only a further extension of you after all. So when your body and your soul have spoken and are ignored, the next messenger to come into play will be your circumstances. These consist of relationships, house, country, work, recreation, and so on.

Do these messengers always act in the same order?

No. Sometimes the body speaks before the environment, and vice versa. But the soul always speaks first.

Please understand that within your world, timing is crucial, as this is the model in which you operate. (Or most of the time, anyway!) So the point is: do not allow time to overtake you. You need to ensure that you are its master, by allowing yourself a balance without its dictates. Forge not a bond between yourself and fate - for fate is merely the caretaker when consciousness is absent.

I had also been attending various short courses and activities at the University of the Third Age, and had run a garden club and courses on dowsing. Then wifi came to the U3A building and I had to bow out. My food swap ended for the same reason, after eight years. Now I had to contend with wifi in buildings, cell phones on people and the radiation from phone towers, which were springing up like mushrooms.

If I allowed myself to be exposed to these I would have a wide range of symptoms, depending on the frequency, length of exposure and what part of my body was exposed to the radiation. My thinking and emotion would be affected, as well as circulation, digestion, eyes, heart and sleep. I would sometimes feel fine at the time, then be so fatigued for days that I had to stay in bed.

My ears rang all the time, and I could not meditate. This reminded me of my mother who, in her last home, suddenly could neither receive a clear television signal nor meditate. This turned out to be due to the new low voltage light bulb that the management had installed above her bed. Once that was replaced, she could meditate again and the television reception was back to normal.

With the rest of humanity, I am a small part of nature. There is no division, no hierarchy. We are all part of the Earth and made of the stars. As a sensitive part of nature, I am affected by the exponential increase in radio-frequency radiation in which we are bathing ourselves. It is far from our natural environment. We are electrical beings through and through, tuned to the resonant Earth frequency of around 7.83 Hz. Now, for the sake of supposed convenience, and profits for some, our communications systems have shot us and all our companion species, gradually up into 3.5 GHz and higher. 1 GHz equals 1 billion Hz. We have increased the intensity of the 7.83 Hz of nature by billions. Our revered wifi operates at 2.4 billion Hz, 5 billion Hz or even more. So how can we expect things to remain the same? Climate, trees, bees, birds, insects, whales, humans… It only takes common sense to see that our whole ecosphere, with everything in it, must be affected. Microwaves raise temperature. Non-ionizing radiation affects human, plant and animal health in numerous ways. This is no supposition. It is clearly shown by over 10,000 peer-reviewed studies, denied and defiled by those who stand to profit from this industry, and from the future it aims towards.

When immunity is affected and the organism weakened, whether it is a tree, a butterfly or a human, it succumbs to disease more readily. We know that this radiation increases mold growth, so what might it do to other simple forms of life such as what we call germs and viruses? When I read of colonies of birds dying, colony collapse disorder in bees, vast numbers of whales beaching themselves, and the plagues of illness now besetting humanity, I am reminded of those early visions I had of a world first without birds, then without life. And I only hope that at some stage before it is too late we will collectively see sense, and realize that survival of life is more essential than convenience or money.

Over aeons of time species have come and gone on this planet, and maybe it is time for mankind to fade back into the mists, but on this occasion he would take most other species with him, which would seem a terrible waste.

In his large book, **The Invisible Rainbow**, a third of which is compiled of references, Arthur Firstenberg describes the history of electricity, beset from the outset with corruption for the sake of profit. It makes a very eye-opening read. Since 2018, Arthur has administered an International Appeal to stop 5G on Earth and in Space, now with hundreds of thousands of signatories, many of whom are scientists, doctors and environmental organizations.

Arthur's latest move is to encourage people to give up their smartphones. We actually survived very well before they came along, and I ran my business successfully for all those years with neither a cell phone nor a website. Before satellites showed us where we were, we used eyes, common sense, maps and compasses if necessary. There has in many ways been a global outsourcing of intelligence, resilience and patience to technology.

The addiction to social media, cell phones and the internet has been astonishingly recent and sudden, as has the global increase in anxiety, depression, suicide, and so many physical illnesses. As a health professional, I studied many diseases back in the late 60's to early 70's. Neurodegenerative conditions such as Parkinsons were virtually non-existent in people under the age of sixty, as were strokes. Now young people are being afflicted by Parkinsons and strokes. Guillain Barre was an extremely rare condition. Now it is quite commonly diagnosed, and my father was one of its victims. Peer-reviewed studies have shown the non-ionising radiation used in wireless communications causes neuropsychiatric changes. Perhaps this could be an explanation for the sudden proliferation of autism and the increase in dementia.

While we point accusingly at emissions from cows and fossil fuels, why is no-one pointing in the same way at emissions from smart phones, phone towers and now 5G satellites? Katie Singer wrote a book called *The Electronic Silent Spring*, reporting the problematic effects of electrification and wireless devices, and looking at solutions. Her studies have high-lighted the vast quantity of energy used in supporting online gaming, or movie streaming; the inhumanity involved in cobalt mining needed for phones; and the mountains of e-waste generated by obsolete phones. She believes that if she is not aware she is part of the problem, then she can't be part of the solution. Her website is called *Our Web of Inconvenient Truths*.

There are many over the world trying their best to halt this pattern, while so many of us 'canaries' merely try to live our lives as best we can despite it. And a far greater number with physical or mental disorders are not even aware they too are 'canaries'.

'Our entire much-praised technological progress, and civilization generally, could be compared to an axe in the hand of a pathological criminal.'

– Albert Einstein, in a letter to H. Zangger, 1917

A Forced Retreat and a Maelstrom Mind

I was forced to drop out of ordinary life. No more entertainment venues or restaurants, no more spending nights away, public buildings or public transport. No more travel. Anywhere people gathered I had to avoid. Wifi was now ubiquitous. Life became limited mostly to walks, gardening at home and researching online. Friends became limited to those who could or would cater to my strange needs. I had to go inward instead of outward. Perhaps life was giving me a rest. Perhaps not.

> Just be yourself, as you are at this time. That is all that is ever asked of you, and no more. Neither try to change yourself; nor to add to yourself. However subtracting from your ideas of yourself may be useful. Allow all your ideas of yourself to fade into the everlasting present. To merge into this moment. Allow it - make no effort. Within that infinite present all is possible and all is created. Effort only shuts doors for you. It hampers the moment from fully expressing itself as it wants to. Allow life to play through you without the barriers of the mind. If you allow it, life will lead you exactly where you need to go, while you merely watch the process.
>
> This is all so different from the messages going around about how we create our world - The Secret, all the motivational courses, etc.
>
> They are all quite true, for those who need these experiences. There is a theory and a method for each and every one. For you the method is to renounce all methods and practise being. Surrender. Others might need to experience their power. You know yours already and need no proof of it. You do not need to set goals and

see them manifest themselves. This lesson is already learned. The particular learning you have designed for yourself at this time is about letting go. It is not that anyone is right or anyone is wrong. Different methods suit different folks at different stages.

Without the busyness of work or a social life I had to come face to face with all my confusions. How to integrate what I had experienced? I had seen the perfection that underlies and pervades this apparently imperfect world. I had felt absolute life, yet didn't always feel that vitality. I had experienced myself as infinite, yet still identified as a person. I identified as a person, yet knew I was not separate – that the same power animates all of life. And what did it mean that I had had all those multidimensional connections? I was still evidently getting caught up in story.

Maelstrom

Maelstrom it is
Inside this head
One way signs and no U turns
Vie for direction
Within time
While timelessness
Waits patiently by
For the memory of Being
To be
Gently descended upon.

Online Gurus, Kindred Spirits and Minds that Create Time

So, still being unable to meditate as I used to, I turned to my trusty friend, the wired world wide web. And there I found numerous gurus and spiritual teachers expounding on their perceptions of reality and truth. I watched videos of Mooji, Adyashanti, Rupert Spira, Francis Lucille and many others. Some revered teachers, like Ramana Maharshi, Nisargadatta Maharaj, and Papaji have passed on and are represented online by valuable old videos. Each contributed a few puzzle pieces.

Buddha at the Gaspump was probably my most consulted site. Here different 'awakening' (and often deeply awakened) people are interviewed by Rick Archer weekly. There are hundreds of these interviews, examining every angle of spirituality, spiritual traditions, experiences and research.

Every now and then in listening to these people, there was a recognition and an 'aha!' as another puzzle piece fell into place. I recognised my process in theirs, and at last could start to create a map of the territory I had traversed. I began to reorient myself, and at last had some language for what I had experienced. I felt the presence of kindred spirits all over the world, a few of whom I contacted.

And of course I read all the books on the process of enlightenment I could get my hands on, though I had to stop visiting the library when their system changed to a radio frequency based one. 'Enlightenment', 'self-realization' and 'awakening' are words often used interchangeably, though some traditions may see subtle differences between them.

> If you stay in Now, your goals will appear before you on time!
>
> What about when I hear no internal directions?
>
> Sometimes you choose not to hear them as they are not to your liking.

So am I getting directions all the time from my higher self if I listen?

Yes. You are guided by the Universe if you are open to it. Failing this, you must be guided by your mind.

Is there no compromise? Can the mind not be in tune with the Universe?

The mind believes it has a life of its own. It believes it is separate from the Universe and must look after your interests. Once the mind has surrendered to the higher power, understanding there really is no other, the messages of the Universe play through the mind. This is when there is no sense of separation. Then it is quite safe to follow the mind, as the mind has become the servant of the soul. While it is trying to be the master, it can only destroy. It cannot ever destroy anything of value. But it can prolong the journey to truth. Time is elongated by the mind. Once the mind is the servant, there is no time. The timeless is the realm of the present, in which the Universe plays.

Undoing Knots and Removing Old Clothes

I learnt a few Hindu terms, which made so much sense to me. One was 'samskara'. Although there are various different definitions of this word to be found, a commonly used meaning is a blockage or impression in the energy system, caused by emotions or beliefs attached to prior experiences. A bit like scarring in the energy field of the body.

In a way I had seen these dealt with through psychotherapy when I had worked in acute psychiatry. Talking until some old issues were mentally resolved was time-consuming and I am not sure how often it actually effected a bodily release of the energy pattern trapped there. With that energy still there, the same old stories and reactions would continue to be activated by the inevitable triggers of life. However treating the psychiatrically ill with drugs seemed to do nothing towards releasing old emotions, merely changing body chemistry to produce different effects, including unwanted side-effects.

In the spiritual healing work I had done, on myself and many others, I had often been able to see these energy blockages, and once seen, there were usually quick simple ways to release them. Methods like EFT (emotional freedom technique) are useful for this, as are forms of body and breath work. Carefully supervised use of such psychoactive plants as ayahuasca or 'magic mushrooms' (psilocybin) can also have cathartic and life-changing effects, hence the recent interest in their use in psychiatry.

To avoid gathering samskaras as an adult, the trick seems to be to allow our feelings to surface and then to naturally subside, without denying them, projecting them onto others, holding on to them or ruminating on them. If allowed to run their natural course, emotions usually do not last long and do not then cause blockages in the bodily energy field. These blockages can cause not only physical illness, but unhelpful habit patterns of belief, thought and behaviour. They limit the freedom of the individual soul to express who it is truly destined to be.

The non-dual way of dealing with unenjoyable feelings may be a little different. Once it has been seen that there is 'no-one in', merely thoughts giving rise to feelings, playing around in the mind, one could ask 'who is feeling this?' or 'who is the one thinking the thought that is giving rise to this feeling?' When it is seen that there is in fact only awareness and no separate person there to feel the feeling, it usually evaporates into peace, light-heartedness or even amusement.

> Every day is a new one - provided the energy from the past has been released.

Those people who have had a glimpse of deeper reality, and are magnetised to go further into clear consciousness, find that their samskaras tend to surface and harass them until they are resolved, by being recognized, accepted and released. I found that too, and all sorts of unconscious content rose up from dark inner dungeons. There would be days of inexplicable grief, sorrow, guilt or frustration, demanding my recognition and release.

In learning about this, my feng shui mind was struck by some parallels. I recalled how, once I had cleared the energy of a place, the occupant would often get sick. There was a corresponding clearing of place and person – one had to match the other. It seems the same is true of body and mind. If the mind gains clarity, that clarity then seeks to be mirrored in the body, requiring some deep clearing and releasing of old emotional scarring. This process can take a long time, often a decade or more.

> It is not useful to put on summer clothes on top of your winter ones. First you must remove the winter clothing, if you want to be ready for summer. And so it is with your lives, attitudes, emotions, perceptions, decisions, relationships and possessions. Each that no longer serves you must be recognized and allowed to leave, gracefully if possible.

An Astonishing Bench and an Invisible Bridge

Online personal and spiritual development webinars and summits had spread like wildfire, and my inbox was inundated with them. Some of them were tempting and I learnt about the latest health and healing research, and research on health effects of radiation. One of my aims was to find the answer to electrosensitivity and share it with others affected as I was.

I was later to discover it is not so simple. Each person is affected for different reasons, in different ways, and no doubt has different lessons to learn before the experience will depart, if indeed it ever does. I tried, among other vain attempts, to use my spiritual understanding to beat my vulnerability. After all, if I am a bit of the power that runs the whole show, how can one little part of this show possibly affect me? It makes no logical sense from that point of view. So I posted up signs in the house to remind myself, 'I am all of it'. But unintegrated cognitive understanding has no power behind it, so that didn't work for long.

I was also still hoping to find out what I was doing on the planet now. Yes I was a mother and grandmother, a gardener, friend, neighbour, poet and so on, but what was my *purpose* now? How was I contributing to life? The idea of having a purpose had recently gained a huge fan-base, in the western world at least! When I had worked in psychiatry, the idea of goal-setting had been all the rage. How interesting the concept has somehow slipped from a person setting goals, to the person having to find the reason for their very existence – their 'purpose'! What about existing for existence's sake? How did that subtle but potentially devastating change happen in our collective psyche?

The concept of 'simply being' has evidently fallen very low in the estimation of our driven materialist world. So is the person without a known purpose now worthless? There is of course also a matter of service, which benefits all who practice it, but I feel we need to watch our language carefully lest it lead us astray. All this is clearer with the benefit of hindsight. On the other hand, I could be ranting here. The reader may decide.

Whenever I asked my channeling, at this point, about my 'purpose' I was told my purpose was to 'be peace.' It would take me a while to accept that!

> The goals of your soul will be met one way or another. There is no getting away from that. You do not have to set goals for this. It will happen regardless. The only goals you might want to set are in regard to smelling the roses along the way, or smoothing another's path. While the first is merely diversion, the second is impossible.
>
> How can I understand this?
>
> You cannot possibly know what is in the path of another and where it leads. In smoothing out one kink in the road you might be causing an avalanche further along. Until you are further evolved yourself you cannot tell. So do only what comes naturally. That way you know you will be doing right. Do not plan. Your plans will emanate from your mind, which knows naught.

Well that was plain speaking!

Retirement was not on my radar yet. I observed a strange pattern happening in my psyche. I would think of some great idea to help the planet, or people and get very enthusiastic. However by day three I would wonder if I was crazy to have thought of such a thing, and all the energy would leave the project! So life was not supporting that role. I was gradually being stripped of my ambitions.

> Our own ideas of action are virtually always in contradiction to life's flow. If they weren't, they would not be experienced as our own!

> *'As soon as the mind pulls out an agenda and decides what needs to change, that's unreality. Life doesn't need to decide who's right and who's wrong. Life doesn't need to know the 'right' way to go because it's going there anyway.'*
>
> **– Adyashanti**

Among the many online treasures I perused, I came across a hypnotherapist who took people back to a time between lives, where they might be able to converse with wise beings about their lives and aims. The idea was that prior to being born we had consulted with higher beings about what we were aiming to achieve in the coming life – what experiences we needed, what we needed to learn, who we needed to interact with and so on. So if we could allow our consciousness to meet these beings again, we could hopefully receive some clues about what we were doing here.

This all sounded like the ticket for me, still reluctant to float in my uncertain state, so I enrolled and had an interesting if inconclusive experience. I was told I must 'build a bridge'. So I took the clues I had been given and channeled further detail about them. What I was told was rather intriguing.

Mankind had so cut itself off from nature that, at some profound etheric level, we had created a sort of invisible but nevertheless real barrier between ourselves and the rest of nature. I was told how to use my shamanic skills to gradually remove this barrier, thereby enabling humanity to more consciously consider and accept nature. I was to build a bridge between man and the rest of nature, in effect. If successful, people would gradually develop more insight into the importance and needs of nature via dreams, intuition and experiences. More conscious behaviour would then hopefully follow.

While I knew I could do what was being asked of me, I had no idea if this was all a massive delusion. It sounded rather grandiose. I was wanting a job, so was I making this up? I asked for a definite sign.

The following day was wild and windy. I drove with my dog to a chemist shop along the coast, and afterwards, despite the weather, had a strong urge to walk Charlie on the beachside path. After a while walking on the narrow path between twisted, windblown banksia trees, we came upon a bench. Most of the benches around there were sponsored by people who have lost loved ones, and they carried a brass plaque to that effect. On arriving at this bench I thought I would sit for a moment and contemplate this new task I had supposedly been allotted. Then I saw the brass plaque. It had the deceased one's name on it, and underneath simply the words *'Build a Bridge'*. There could not have been a clearer confirmation!

So over a few weeks I built that bridge, creating gaps in the barrier we had created, above many densely populated cities of the world. Had I not been asked to do this, I might have regarded it as interfering and not done it, but I had been clearly asked. I have found that often if I stare inwardly at something etheric, it changes towards its natural state. So I focussed on this barrier until each area of focus dissolved, leaving a hole through which man and nature could connect. Eventually one day I watched, as the rest of the now flimsy barrier lifted off by itself, and I knew my job was done. I also returned to that bench several times to see that plaque, which was as solid a part of reality as ever.

Obliging Sandals, Adaptable Daisies, Moses and Kind Rain

'The more in harmony you are with the flow of your own existence, the more magical life becomes.'

– Adyashanti

The apparent miracles still cropped up at unexpected times.

Color was a theme of some:

I had bought a particularly well shaped and comfortable pair of blue thongs (the Australian term for flip flops) on a visit to the Philippines in 2008. These finally died and I looked everywhere for a similar blue comfortable pair. Even online, none were to be found. I already had two flat brown pairs at the back door, and having given up my search, decided to fetch one of those instead.

Imagine my surprise on seeing both pairs had turned blue! I took one pair to the front door and left the other at the back door. After a few days I thought it was a pity I now had no brown thongs, as I quite liked to wear brown sometimes. However the next time I went out the back door, I found that the pair there had again turned brown!

Then there was a flower incident. My lovely neighbour Marj was a gardener like me, and had a soft spot for daisies. At a nursery one day I saw an unusual yellow-pink daisy, and fleetingly imagined Marj would like it. However I didn't buy it. The following day at home I was astonished to see that the flowers on my yellow daisy plant had turned yellow-pink, like the one I had seen at the nursery. I gave Marj a cutting, hoping the new colour would remain if it grew. After a few days my plant went back to its customary yellow flowers.

Several months later I asked Marj if the cutting had grown. Apparently it had not. So she still only had her pink daisy. I commented that it was a pity she didn't also have a yellow one. The following day there were two yellow flowers on her pink daisy bush!

And there were a few water incidents:

My dog and I were walking on the deserted beach and the tide was in. We were about to turn back before we reached the point where the waves met the sea wall. Then suddenly there was a quiet whoosh, and the water receded by about two meters, allowing us to walk on. I felt like Moses! Charlie and I were equally astounded! We walked there and back, then the water whooshed back in again.

For years I have noticed some sort of benevolent relationship with the spirit of rain. When out walking, the skies darken at times and I know rain is imminent. A few drops fall, like warning shots, as I hasten home or to my car. Sometimes these few drops happen for quite some time. Then as soon as I am under cover, the rain unleashes itself and pelts down. This even happens when I am in my garden. The warning drops happen until I am safely inside.

Decades ago I sewed an applique picture honouring earth, air, fire and water, and in recent years I send each a blessing daily when I practice my qi gong. Maybe the spirit of water blesses me back? However I do wonder how much these mini-miracles happen to all of us and pass unnoticed.

And plant miracles:

I have several raised garden beds for growing vegetables. In one I grow dandelions, as a reliable, hardy, nutritious green crop. Noticing how disorderly and crowded these dandelions had become, and how consequently their leaves were smaller, I thought I must soon thin them out. A couple of days later to my utter astonishment I saw they had been neatly thinned out and were now two well-spaced rows of eight each! Surely this must be Pan's doing?

On the nature strip outside my front fence there had long been a patch of 'lawn' that was weeds, since underground plumbing work had been undertaken years ago there. This square had then been sown with grass seeds, but the weeds had conquered the space and it had been a mess ever since. On putting out the bins, I noticed it again and tried spraying the weeds with a harmless weedicide, which didn't work. The weeds merely grinned at me triumphantly.

Then a couple of weeks later I happened to notice a particularly lush green patch of grass on the otherwise rather feeble lawn outside. It was exactly where the weedy square had been! A complete transformation!

I had no choice but to accept a state of not knowing, with all these strange events. There was no way I could be sure of the mechanism of any of them. They had to remain mysteries and I had to be content with that.

'Right now you can allow yourself to experience a very simple sense of not knowing – not knowing what or who you are, not knowing what this moment is, not knowing anything. If you give yourself this gift of not knowing and you follow it, a vast spaciousness and mysterious openness dawns within you. Relaxing into not knowing is almost like surrendering into a big, comfortable chair; you just fall into a field of possibility.'

– Adyashanti

I recalled my father had owned a book called *The Cloud of Unknowing*, a mystical work written by an unknown author in medieval times. I wished I could refer to it.

CHAPTER 19

Living the Mystery

Slow Falling into Timeless Being

Meanwhile I seemed to be quietly but surely undergoing my own transformation. It was now easier to just be, without hankering for some unknown purpose or aiming to save the world in some way. Perhaps most retirees come to this place.

Life had become moment by moment in an ongoing present flow, which expanded to fill my days. I realized that changing my position in space by travel, would not necessarily make me happier. My state arose from inside not outside. Entertainment did not hold as much interest. Peter had rather disparagingly called movies 'a play within a play' and I could now see his point. How could distraction from life be any more interesting than the real thing, which is so utterly extraordinary?

Even the word 'extraordinary' bears some analysis. It holds the implication that most things are 'ordinary'. Yet are they? Nothing is really deeply understood, except perhaps by the profoundly mystical sages. No scientist has a recipe for life itself. Everything around us is made of magic – energy in motion, different for each perceiver. Science continuously has to correct itself, as it finds more which cancels out its prior discoveries. Hypotheses and theories are simply stories within a mystery.

> If you give up all theories what is left?
> Knowing is left. All theories are limited and limiting.

Our lives are an enigmatic riddle.

'There are moments when one feels free from one's own identification with human limitations and inadequacies. At such moments, one imagines that one stands on some spot of a small planet, gazing in amazement at the cold yet profoundly moving beauty of the eternal, the unfathomable: life and death flow into one, and there is neither evolution nor destiny; only being.'
– Albert Einstein, in a letter to Queen Mother Elisabeth of Belgium, 1939

Thoughts cropped up and at times my mind was very busy, but knowing those thoughts were not me, I could usually slip behind them into the peace of being while letting them do their thing.

> Do not revel in your thoughts. Try to see them and catch them in action, when they start. Once they have carried you off on a train

it is harder to stop. Not to step on a train is easier than stepping off a moving one.

When conditioned ideas based on old 'shoulds' cropped up, I would notice them and allow them to fade away. Instead I did what I felt like doing, what came naturally. This did not mean being selfish as much as sensing what felt right to do at the time, rather than following old patterns.

The angst of my old pattern of looking for the 'correct path' was dissolved into the understanding that there isn't one – that we create life as we go along, according to how we respond to what comes our way. We each have different blueprints to discover and live out, and I felt I was closer to mine by simply being true to myself, instead of following my conditioned ideas. This was so much more relaxing.

> Do whatever comes up to do without thinking. Experiment doing it this way and see what happens. Be free. Do not let your mind rule you with thinking. Regard your thinking as a joke. It comes, it disrupts, it goes. That is all. It is never reliable, as it is unstable. You are basing your feelings on what comes up in your mind – this is why they are all over the place. That is how your mind is. Base your feelings rather on what is stable and real.
>
> Observe what comes up in your mind. Laugh at it. It is ridiculous and aimed at keeping you stuck. The mind is afraid of disintegrating. So it does not want you to become aware. It is not on your side. Yet it may be a good servant if you keep it in its place. Be careful not to let it rule you. See it for what it is. Merely a tool that would be king!

Mind Power and Letting Go of Saving the World

I realized that ever since those early visions of a world devoid of life, I had taken on the responsibility of trying to save it, in one way or another. Now I was being shown the best role to take to that end was to be peace, on the inside. *The frequency I broadcast to the world is more important than any action I might perform.*

That sense of responsibility to *do something*, melted off my shoulders. Each of us is unique and plays different roles. This is simply the role I am now allotted, the one everything else in my life has led to.

Through much of my life I had been not only a warrior, but a worrier. Now I clearly saw the wisdom of Mark Twain's famous observation: "I've lived through a thousand tragedies, none of which actually happened!" All that wasted energy! And through focussing on possible problems, I had probably succeeded in creating many. Living in the expansive moment of complete uncertainty is so much easier, on body and mind.

My relationship to my body changed too. Symptoms would come and go without so much worry about them. It helps to know that my body is my instrument but not what I am. The body is an exquisitely brilliant organism, which knows how to correct and balance itself, if allowed to by our thoughts, habits and environs. I had noticed how quick the body is to respond to the mind.

Many stories are attributed to the Dalai Lama, including one of him waking up with a painful knee. To deal with that condition, he decided he needed to climb a mountain that day, which he did. It seems he did not allow the concept of a knee problem in his consciousness, and thus healed the knee. Thoughts of vulnerability to illness tend to give rise to it. Whereas confidence that the body can overcome outside influences tends to have that effect. This body of mine is still affected by radiofrequency radiation, but less so, despite more of it.

Dr Bruce Lipton's classic book, **The Biology of Belief,** explains the influence of epigenetics. The genes are not necessarily as defining as we thought they were. Our thoughts and environs are the master of our genes, and these days with the right help from those who understand this, people are healing themselves of all sorts of supposedly incurable conditions. Dr Joe Dispenza works with vast numbers of people to this end and has written many books – one called *Becoming Supernatural.*

Lynne McTaggart, an American journalist, writer and researcher, has written much on the healing power of people in groups. She has conducted experiments with large international groups of people and scientists, which have demonstrated that our intention is very potent, and can be used to reduce crime, clean water, promote peace and heal people. One of her books is called **The Power of Eight,** and is a result of her discovery that small groups of people with intent to heal one of them, usually effect beneficial changes. Distance between the people is irrelevant, so most of these groups are online.

What surprised Lynne most was discovering that those who sent the healing intent seemed to often benefit as much as the recipient. There was a mirror effect.

Think not problematic thoughts. Make your thoughts only your intents. Thus will you not waste a thought.

Do my thoughts automatically create?

Of course they do.

All is One, All is Well and a Cosmic Body

I want to understand better how my infinite awareness nature interfaces with my limited body-mind.

Allow it to be the master of your body-mind. This way your whole life will be magic. When the body-mind is identified with, life is very pedestrian and predictable, apart from sudden shocks. Have no expectations and no fear, and life will unfold as a colourful blossom.

Surely my creativity wants expression? Yet I am doing nothing in that vein.

If it really wanted expression you would be. All is well. Be in the moment, as it is. Do what comes before you - no more, no less.

You are only an instrument for life to play through.

The confusions I had about how to integrate the absolute and the relative, the transcendental and the mundane were ironed out gradually. Some Advaita teachers place much emphasis on the unreality, dreamlike nature and even non-existence of the body and world. This understanding might be a necessary step on the road to truth, but if clung to, can have the effect of supporting concepts of duality rather than the non-dual truth of integrated oneness. It can also lead to a sense of meaninglessness, depersonalization and disconnection from life, even depression. Believing that only the 'absolute' or transcendent is real and matters, can also lead to many relationship problems. People like to feel they matter.

The answer to the riddle is contained in the Zen Buddhist phrase: 'Samsara is nirvana'.

The repetitive, mundane world of suffering that we perceive, is pervaded always by the bliss of the sublime, in an inseparable dance of oneness. They were never apart. All is in the one and the one is in all. As the Buddha said: 'Emptiness is form and form is emptiness.' As Hindus say: 'Atman is Brahman'. The individual and the universal are one. Any sense of separation is illusory. Nothing is outside the Self. The inner and the outer are dissolved into one.

This understanding turns the world from mundane to miraculous, and helped me to see that there is nowhere 'up there' or 'out there' to aim for. This is it! *What* we already are and *where* we already are is all we could wish for, if we allow ourselves to see it. We are still each unique. Every role played, no matter how it looks, every feeling felt is sacred. As Peter used to say, 'There are no mistakes.'

All we need to do is be ourselves. That does not mean the conditioned self with all its ego-driven machinations, but the real self, so often hidden to us by the conditioned layers imposed. Yet even those layers are a valid part of the play, and their gradual dissolution is assured over time – usually life-times.

Recently I tried an exercise which is part of a course of the Buddha's teachings, run by a friend of mine. This exercise simply involves closing one's eyes and looking in at the body. To my surprise, I couldn't do it! On closing my eyes and focussing in, my body seemed to be replaced by the cosmos. There was no sense of a body at all! This was a change, and showed me that development continues whether we do much about it or not, once we are on this spiritual roller coaster towards inner freedom.

Beloved Beliefs and Invisible Ships

And as for all the realms I had dealt with which we seldom see: they are around all of us all the time in unseen layers. Most people have probably had glimpses, but, according to literature I found, to have more than a few glimpses one needs to develop one's 'sixth sense'. I wonder if a prerequisite is also to have an open mind. Believing anything at all is possible surely enables the apparently impossible to happen in our own experience. Our beliefs are a fundamental force in our lives, enabling inclusion or exclusion of events.

In my case I was lucky to have some weird experiences and thoughts early on which were not drowned by a dogmatic family. So I was wide open to impossible possibilities!

It has been postulated that, when the first tall colonial ships entered Australian waters, they were initially not seen by the indigenous people, as there had been no precedent for such apparitions. I wonder if this power of our beliefs to shape our experience could be partly due to the phenomenon of cognitive dissonance.

Cognition refers to our thoughts, attitudes and values. We feel a greater or lesser degree of discomfort when two of them are incompatible with each other. For instance we might think talk of UFOs is utter nonsense. But then we might see one. The mind can work very fast to solve the discomfort problem. Perceiving the UFO might well be blocked from our consciousness, as it just does not fit our mindset. Another example: we have total faith that the government is looking after us. Then they advocate something that is bad for us. In this case we might refuse to see the latter, as the former is such a long held belief.

It takes humility and courage to see that former fondly held beliefs were maybe not the whole story, and to allow into the mind a new version.

Living the Mystery

'Unthinking respect for authority is the greatest enemy of truth.'
– Albert Einstein, 1901

Perhaps this could apply too, to the authority we grant to our long-cherished beliefs?

Cognitive dissonance, or maybe simply personal ego investment, possibly explains the persistence of hypotheses still held as true in various fields of science, long after they are disproved. Quantum physics causes such a problem to Newtonian physics that it is still not as respected and widely taught as it might be. We still supposedly live in a solid material world, unaffected by any observer, more than a hundred years after that has been soundly disproved!

The notion that we live as separate beings in a solid material world has shaped our modern medical, educational, and economic systems too. However it seems in all supposedly stuck systems, other more enlightened ways are gradually infiltrating, and will hopefully take over as the old systems crumble, despite cognitive dissonance, ego and habit.

'Concepts that have proven useful in ordering things easily achieve such authority over us that we forget their earthly origins and accept them as unalterable givens.'
– Albert Einstein, 1916

Patterns, The Wise Ones, Peace and The Birth of a Book

Not only are we one consciousness playing as many, and viewing from billions of viewpoints, but there are realms within realms in the same play, doing the same thing. What opens the flower is what grows my hair and what animates an elephant. One infinite Life plays through all these forms – visible and invisible to us. And each of these forms has a unique contribution to make in how that Life is expressed.

The forms come and go in a never-ending pattern of recycling, while the recycler is unchanged. Once we identify more with that permanent recycler – Life itself – than with the temporary forms that are recycled, we are freer to be the creative parts of nature we were originally designed to be. And then, it seems, nature responds, reaching out a friendly hand.

I realized that I have no idea really how my nails grow or how planets turn, so why would I need to know how all the other strange phenomena of my life work? It's all simply nature weaving its magic, and I too am nature. I am looking at so many incidents as miracles, but why should these inexplicable events be any more miraculous than a bee buzzing, a sunset or the moon?

Due to the confident hubris of science, we assume we have so much taped, but we do not yet understand life or consciousness at all. Many, if not most scientists still attribute consciousness to the brain, when new research, like old mysticism, indicates we swim in it, and in fact, there may well be nothing else. It is all miraculous.

'If God created the world, his primary concern was certainly not to make its understanding easy for us.'

– Albert Einstein

Indigenous cultures have long held far more understanding of these essential mysteries than most of us. Hopefully we are becoming more ready to learn from them and their respectful connection with nature.

How much of nature we have lost, in only a few industrialized centuries. Economic rationalism, consumerism, revolving fashion, individualism and competition take us far from our natural states of peace, simplicity and respect for mother Earth, on whom we utterly depend. Now surely the time has come to slow down, quieten down, and listen to what the Earth and our own souls are trying to tell us.

There is much about my life I will never understand with the mind. But I am now more content not to know. I am content to live as a spirit among spirits, in a magical and unpredictable universe, knowing none of us ever die, and the possibilities are infinite. The phrase 'it is as it is' seems a peaceful one to live with.

---

*'The universe is an inexhaustible celebration
of ultimate mystery!'*

– Brian Swimme

So I enjoy drifting from day to day with few plans. However, as they say, life abhors a vacuum. Maybe that is why I received an email meant for someone else called Paula. The email was offering me a place in a writing circle. The wise sender, realizing the 'mistake' was made by the Universe, went with the flow, as did I in accepting. I had meant to write this book for at least a decade, and this invitation prompted me to begin.

Another Day

Who wouldn't want another day
In this crazy cacophony
Of contrast

Who wouldn't want another lick
At this rainbow ice-cream
Of existence

Where on blue revolving
Dangling sphere
Man's mad machinations
Are lovingly encircled
By Nature's kind green graces

Where sky-floating gulls push back
Against the wind
And the guns of war beat at
The bells of peace

Where horses gallop
With manes like ribbons
And snails creep
Into dark wet spaces

Where brick and metal soar into clouds
And dogs let their tongues hang

Where ships conquer water
Planes conquer air
And man mistakenly
Tries to conquer Nature

Fish cavort hidden
From crowded cities
And worms dance quietly
Beneath the brown

Where waves caress shorelines
And mountains rise God-like
Birth and death revolve
And churches call to prayer

Skies turn dark, then light
As clouds rush by
Then dark again and water pelts

Spring and the perfume of freesias
Autumn and fire-scattered ground
Who wouldn't want another day of this?

www.ingramcontent.com/pod-product-compliance
Lightning Source LLC
Chambersburg PA
CBHW051333110526
44591CB00026B/2984